PLAYING *for an* AUDIENCE *of* ONE

PLAYING *for an* AUDIENCE *of* ONE

*Learning to Live
for the
Approval of Jesus*

JOSHUA BROOKS

Pleasant W rd
A Division of WINEPRESS PUBLISHING

Pleasant Word (a division of WinePress Publishing, PO Box 428, Enumclaw, WA 98022) functions only as book publisher. As such, the ultimate design, content, editorial accuracy, and views expressed or implied in this work are those of the author.

Unless otherwise noted, all Scriptures are taken from the *Holy Bible, New International Version*®, *NIV*®. Copyright © 1973, 1978, 1984 by the International Bible Society. Used by permission of Zondervan. All rights reserved.

ISBN 13: 978-1-4141-1131-5
ISBN 10: 1-4141-1131-2
Library of Congress Catalog Card Number: 2007908463

CONTENTS

ACKNOWLEDGMENTS

I'VE GOT TO begin by thanking my Warm Beach church family. Your response to the "Playing for an Audience of One" messages confirmed my sense that God was calling me to write this book. Seeing so many of you take to heart what it means to live for Jesus' approval has been an unbelievable joy. More than that, thank you for being the community where I am continuing to work out what it means for me to play for an "Audience of One."

Thank you, Pat, for absorbing more of the ministry load so I could take this sabbatical. You have truly modeled what it looks like for a pastor to check his ego at the door for the good of the body of Christ.

Jason, your willingness to painstakingly proofread every chapter and give feedback was a huge point of encouragement to me. Thank you, too, to so many of you who loaned me your eyes and insights at various points during the rough draft phase.

Brandon and Angie, even more than the money, the way you approached me with the offer to underwrite the expense of this book was another confirmation that God would see this project through to completion. Thank you for your investment. I pray that it will pay dividends for the kingdom.

Amanda, what can I say? Your tireless reading (and re-reading) of multiple drafts was a love gift to me. Your prayers and encouragement for me to live out God's calling mean more than you'll ever know. I love you.

Finally, if there are people who get something out of this book, fantastic. But ultimately, this book is dedicated to the One who called me to write it. Where my ability to communicate clearly and compellingly has fallen short (and I'm sure it has at points), my prayer, Lord Jesus, is that my heart's desire to be obedient has brought You joy.

A Note from the Author

I WAS SEVENTEEN years old when I committed the rest of my life to following Jesus. I had all sorts of ideas about what God would want for and from me. But just about the first thing He did was tap me on the shoulder, and call out my tendency to try and make myself look good in other people's eyes. Managing one's reputation is standard operating procedure in high school. And as I soon discovered, it was fairly typical among Christians, too. However, as I also learned, the Holy Spirit wasn't interested in me settling for what was common practice–even if it was common among His people.

I remember God's still small voice saying to me, *'If you stop jockeying for people's approval and worrying about what other people think about you, I will guard your reputation and allow you to enjoy the freedom that comes from living for My approval alone.'*

It seemed odd that this would be one of the first things God would say to me. I figured there had to be more important things He wanted to do in and through me. But seventeen years later, I'm as convinced as ever that living for Jesus' approval is His highest calling on my life. Everything flows from this.

I certainly haven't arrived when it comes to playing for an Audience of One. Some days I still feel like that insecure seventeen year old who cares too much about what people are thinking of me. But more often than not I really am experiencing the joy and freedom that comes from simply living for the approval of Jesus.

My prayer is that in reading this book, God might use it to help you experience this same joy and freedom.

Joshua Brooks
Warm Beach, Washington
February 2008

THE STAKES ARE HIGHER THAN YOU THINK

> *"The trouble with so many people is that the voice of their neighbors sounds louder in their ears than the voice of God."*
>
> —H.G. Wells

IN 1520, MARTIN LUTHER was summoned by Emperor Charles V to appear at the Imperial Assembly in the city of Worms. He faced charges of teaching doctrine that contradicted some of the traditional tenets of the Roman Church. Luther's friends tried to dissuade him from going to Worms, warning him of the impending danger waiting for him there. But Luther unswervingly held his ground, replying, "You can expect from me everything except fear or recanting. I shall not flee, much less renounce my convictions."

Luther set his face like a flint toward Worms. "Not go to Worms!" he said. "I shall go to Worms though there were as many devils as tiles on the roofs."

When the proceedings began, Counselor Eck held up Luther's writings and called upon him to recant: "Will Luther reject his books and the errors they contain?"

The father of the Protestant Reformation then answered with the words that would ring through history: "Unless I can be instructed and convinced with evidence from the Holy Scriptures or with open, clear, and distinct grounds of reasoning, then I cannot and will not recant, because it is neither safe nor wise to act against conscience. God help me. Amen. Here I stand, I cannot do otherwise!"[1]

We love stories of courage and conviction. We're inspired by the underdog who stands toe to toe with the giant, resolving to die, if need be, for the sake of the truth. There are two reasons. First of all, we inherently know that this is the way we're supposed to live. Even those of us who feel handcuffed by fear know that ultimately it is "neither safe nor wise to act against conscience." And the truth is most of us wish we had more courage to live our lives with this kind of boldness.

The other reason we love these stories is we have a sense that the stakes are high. It's not just the health of our own soul that's on the line when we take a stand. When we take the high road amidst opposition and peer pressure, we really can change our world for the better. It's always been that way:

- Martin Luther King, Jr., helped topple the strongholds of racism and prejudice in America by staying true to his vision, "I have a dream!"
- Patrick Henry inspired a fledgling nation of farmers to take on the most sophisticated military the world had ever known, shouting, "Give me liberty or give me death!"
- Mary, a peasant teenager, faced the criticism and shame of a pregnancy out of wedlock, agreeing to give birth to the Messiah, and saying, "I am the Lord's servant. May it be to me as you have said" (Luke 1:38).
- Esther used her influence to rescue the Jewish people, risking her life and saying, "I will go to the king, even though it is against the law. And if I perish, I perish" (Est. 4:16).
- David, a young shepherd boy, ignored the fearful voices of his fellow Israelites and fought Goliath, the heavyweight champion of the Philistine army, saying, "You come against me with sword and spear, but I come against you in the name of the Lord!" (1 Sam. 17:45).

- Moses, a stuttering, eighty-year-old fugitive, stood up against the military superpower of the fifteenth century B.C., proclaiming, "Let my people go!" (Ex. 5:1).

Granted, the stands we take in life may not change the face of the whole world. After all, very few of us live in a context that resembles that of these famous historical figures. But that doesn't mean we can't significantly impact our little corner of the world. Living out our convictions really does have the potential to make a kingdom difference in our sphere of influence. Regardless of how seemingly ordinary we might feel about the roles we play in life, the stands we take matter. *The stakes are higher than we think:*

- For the employee, who is willing to stand up to his co-workers (and even his superiors) when the ethical high road is forsaken.
- For parents, who long for their children's affections, but resolve to discipline them anyway, even though they may incur feelings of resentment from them.
- For the pastor, who pursues the vision God has called him to despite what some of the people in the church might think about him.
- For the single mom, who keeps taking her children to church, regardless of the sting she feels every time she gets asked, "So where is your husband?"
- For the teenager, who speaks out about her spiritual convictions at school even in the face of mockery and ridicule from her peers.

Unfortunately, we don't always live up to who we want to be. I wish I didn't care what people thought about me, but sometimes I do. I wish it took outright persecution before I began to shy away from speaking forth my convictions. But sometimes it doesn't take much peer pressure at all before I find myself going the way of people pleasing.

After all, I want people to like me.

Some of us avoid speaking out about what we believe because we can't stand the thought of someone thinking badly about us. Others are inclined to people-please because if we were to speak the truth in certain situations, it might lead to an uncomfortable confrontation. That might produce pain or resentment in other people, and we don't want to risk losing their affections and approval. So we play it safe.

The root cause for our inclination to hedge our bets and people-please is that we are more concerned with what people think than with what God thinks. As I re-read that last sentence, I wince at what feels like the blunt edge of a sword, but there is no way to soften the blow. For many of us, our ears have become attuned to the opinions of people, all the while becoming deaf to the voice of God. As H.G. Wells once said, "The trouble with so many people is that the voice of their neighbors sounds louder in their ears than the voice of God."[2]

I am all too aware of this people-pleasing tendency in my own life. I spend far too much time trying to figure out what people think about me. I find myself mentally calculating what my "stock" is worth on the trading floor of public opinion. I wonder how certain decisions I make will affect my reputation in the eyes of other people. I don't even have to be intentional about thinking these kinds of thoughts. My mind just naturally drifts this way. And I'm not alone. As a pastor, I daily encounter what a struggle this issue is for many followers of Jesus. It's an epidemic that is plaguing the church, crippling many of us from living in the freedom God desires for us.

Why do so many of us long for approval from other people? Is our craving for affirmation just some baseless neurosis? Is it simply the result of low self-esteem? No. The fact of the matter is we were created with an approval-sized void that only can be filled by the One who made us. Most of us mentally ascend to this truth. Unfortunately, we still settle for a shadow of the real thing, grasping for glory and affirmation from other human beings instead of from the One who wants to give it to us.

It may sound unspiritual, and even self-centered, but God actually *wants* to give us glory. C.S. Lewis writes:

> When I began to look into this matter I was shocked to find such different Christians as Milton, Johnson, and Thomas Aquinas taking

heavenly glory quite frankly in the sense of fame or good report. But not fame conferred by our fellow creatures—fame with God, approval…by God. And then, when I had thought it over, I saw that this view was scriptural; nothing can eliminate from the parable the divine accolade, "Well done, thou good and faithful servant." With that, a good deal of what I had been thinking all my life fell down like a house of cards. I suddenly remembered that no one can enter heaven except as a child; and nothing is so obvious in a child—not in a conceited child, but a good child—as its great and undisguised pleasure in being praised. Not only in a child, either, but even in a dog or a horse. Apparently what I had mistaken for humility had, all these years, prevented me from understanding what is in fact the humblest, the most childlike, the most creaturely of pleasures—nay, the specific pleasure of the inferior: the pleasure of a beast before men, a child before it's father, a pupil before his teacher, a creature before its Creator. I am not forgetting how horribly this most innocent desire is parodied in our human ambitions, or how quickly, in my own experience, the lawful pleasure of praise from those whom it was my duty to please turns into the deadly poison of self-admiration. But I thought I could detect a moment—a very, very short moment—before this happened, during which the satisfaction of having pleased those whom I rightly loved and rightly feared was pure. And that is enough to raise our thoughts to what may happen when the redeemed soul, beyond all hope and nearly beyond belief, learns at last that she has pleased Him whom she was created to please.[3]

This is what we were made for…

The response to the siren voices that seduce you into seeking after your neighbors' approval is to learn to play for an Audience of One: to raise your thoughts to the glory that only God can confer upon you, and attune your ears to hear His voice amidst the competing voices that vie for your attention. This is the antidote for the people-pleasing disease. You don't have to live under the tyranny of others' opinions another day. In fact, as you learn to play for an Audience of One, you will begin to experience the thrill of living your life the way God intended you to live. You no longer have to live in bondage to what other people think. Your days more and more will be marked by freedom, courage, conviction, and the kind of peace that allows you to sleep well at night, knowing you have been true to who God has called you to be.

My hunch is that you want to play for an Audience of One. Most followers of Jesus do. But I also know merely being told to do so won't get me there. For the most part, I already know what I'm supposed to do. As the eighteenth century doctor Samuel Johnson said, "People need to be reminded more often than they need to be instructed."[4]

What I need are poignant reminders that jog my memory about why it's worth it to keep striving after this goal. What I need are stories of real people whose courageous resolve in the face of opposition inspire me to live for something greater than public approval. What I need are biblical examples and everyday illustrations that show me what it looks like to play for an Audience of One. So if you're like me, and you're frustrated and weary of settling for a shadow of the real thing, then turn the page. Let's learn to play for an Audience of One.

Chapter 2

"THOUGH NONE GO WITH ME, STILL I WILL FOLLOW"

*"To sin by silence when we should protest
makes cowards of men."*
—Abraham Lincoln

OFTEN TIMES I have a tendency to talk too much. Like many pastors, there have certainly been occasions when I've missed my stop. Unfortunately, there are other times when I've gotten very quiet precisely when I needed to speak up—as in the following story.

The denominational leadership had just presented the state of the work address to hundreds of us pastors. The basic gist of their speech was that we were going to approach the matter of church membership differently in the future. Traditionally, our denomination has defined its membership by a list of external rules. Some of us have even learned a little ditty to remind ourselves of The List: "Don't drink, smoke, chew, or go with girls who do."

But the denominational leaders were painting a picture of a new day, one in which legalism would no longer drive the membership discussion. The mantra throughout their presentation was that *membership in the local church would be as nearly as possible synonymous with entrance into the body of Christ.* In other words, becoming a follower of Jesus would be the only prerequisite for someone becoming a member of one of our

7

local churches. From there, the Holy Spirit, solid biblical preaching, and the discipleship process would be trusted to bring about the changes that needed to take place in each new believer's life. The majority of pastors were ecstatic about this paradigm shift. Personally, I've hungered for years to get away from a membership list of rules that only serves to mislead people as to what Christianity is all about.

Following the address, we were invited to respond to what we had heard. Many asked questions in order to confirm that we were being given the freedom to bring into membership people who, for example, drink alcohol. But it soon became clear that the denomination was not ready to change the membership guidelines when it came to that particular issue. The leadership wanted to talk about reforming our denomination's legalistic bent, but they were not quite ready to take steps to correct it when it came to the alcohol issue.

I could sympathize with the leadership regarding their dilemma. They truly wanted to move our denomination away from the kind of legalism that was quenching the Spirit's power in the life of the church. I believe their desire in this matter was sincere. But (though I don't presume to know their hearts) they also seemed concerned about our denomination's more traditional constituents perceiving them as having abandoned our emphasis on holiness. If this was indeed a real fear, it was an understandable one. There are those within our denominational family who genuinely believe that partaking of any amount of alcohol or tobacco will so junk up the temple of the Holy Spirit that God is unwilling—perhaps unable—to work through such a vessel. I know: I've talked to a few of them.

I've shared with these folks how people like C. S. Lewis, whom God used mightily and whose writing they quote, smoked a pipe and drank beer at his local pub. I enjoy watching what happens next as they perform intellectual gymnastics, trying to reconcile C.S. Lewis with their deeply held conviction that God's Spirit couldn't possibly work this powerfully through someone who drank alcohol.

A disclaimer is probably required at this point. I am certainly not oblivious to the damage that alcohol can cause. Most of the members of my family have had their lives devastated by alcohol. I've experienced its ravaging effects up close and personally. I still have occasional nightmares related to growing up in a home with an alcoholic father. That's why I've chosen not to drink. That's also why as a pastor I strongly encourage people to weigh the minimal benefits of drinking over and against the incredibly high risks involved. But (and this is a very big "but") I have no scriptural authority to mandate that this is *the* biblical position to take on the alcohol issue. More importantly, I could never biblically justify calling people to abstain from alcohol as a prerequisite to following Jesus and joining the body of Christ. The Bible just doesn't go there. And where the Scriptures are not crystal clear, we should avoid making black and white declarations. Otherwise, we slip into legalism.

The denominational leaders wanted our church to be free of legalism. But there was no way to get there without offending those who might question a new membership code. So just as I've done at many points in my life, the leadership tried their best to walk the fence. Even more tragic than their fence walking, though, was the fact that in a room full of pastors, nobody seemed willing to call them on it. Finally, one pastor had the courage to stand up and challenge the notion that membership in the local church could be both 'synonymous with becoming a Christian' and 'contingent upon abstaining from alcohol.'

The leaders were noticeably taken aback by the pastor's comment. So they reiterated the vision of putting legalism behind us, and tried to sound convincing about this "new" era we were entering. But they didn't back away from the language of abstaining from alcohol. Still standing, the pastor confessed again his confusion regarding the logical basis of their position, since Scripture never claims that abstaining from alcohol is a prerequisite for becoming a follower of Jesus. The pastor's question was met with the same response, without any further clarification about how this new membership model could be reconciled to what Scripture says.

And with that, the discussion was over.

Despite the fact that the integrity of the Scriptures and the life of the church were at stake, not one other pastor was willing to press the issue. There was just a loud silence that filled the room. After all, publicly confronting the leadership about a controversial issue is a risky move that could jeopardize one's professional status and ministerial reputation.

Once the question and answer time was over, a ministry colleague walked up to the pastor who had raised the membership question and said, "Well, if you ever wanted to become bishop, you just shot yourself in the foot!" The pastor simply nodded, noticeably discouraged by his peers' silence.[5]

As the old saying goes, "Silence is golden, but sometimes it's just plain yellow."

The Choice: Approval of God or Affections of People?

Nobody understood the truth of that maxim better than the apostle Paul. He has become one of my heroes in the journey of learning to play for an Audience of One. In particular, it was his letter to the Galatians that first illuminated for me the path of freedom from the people-pleasing disease. Challenged to bow down to the pressure of his ministry peers regarding a critical doctrinal decision, he wrote this:

> Am I now trying to win the approval of men, or of God? Or am I trying to please men? If I were still trying to please men, I wouldn't be a servant of Christ.
>
> —Gal. 1:10

This is really the Scripture that inspired me to start praying about what it meant to play for an Audience of One. The significance of Paul's rhetorical question to the Galatians has only grown in my mind as I've begun to understand the first century context in which he lived out these words. They were written at a hinge point in the life of the church, at a watershed moment when the future of the gospel was at stake. Paul had to make a choice between the approval of God and the affections of people. The implications of his choice would have a ripple effect throughout church history.

The Watershed Issue

In the early days of the church, there were basically two camps with competing views about how the Gentiles could come into a saving relationship with God and fully participate with the people of God:

1. *The Judaizers*, also known as "the circumcision sect," were in the first camp. They were a powerful Christian constituency, and they propagated a version of the gospel that promoted a two-step process for how the Gentiles could be saved. First, the Gentiles needed to say yes to Jesus. Second, they needed to say yes to keeping all of the Law. Essentially, the Judaizers' equation for salvation was: *Grace + Law = Basis for our Salvation.*
   This meant that in order for the Gentiles to be saved and participate in the body of Christ, they needed to be circumcised and keep all of the dietary and table fellowship laws.

2. *Paul* stood on the other side of the theological fence, speaking out against the Judaizers' two-step version of the gospel. He passionately decried the idea that anything needed to be added to grace in order to receive salvation and full membership among God's people. He was convinced that "grace" + "anything" would negate the reality of grace itself. Paul's salvation equation for Jew and Gentile alike was simple: *Grace + Nothing = Basis for our Salvation.*

It's important to remember that Paul was no blonde-haired, blue-eyed, hotdog-eating Gentile. He was a Jew. He grew up under the Law. He diligently studied the Law. He loved the Law. He lived his life in strict adherence to the letter of the Law. In fact, Paul was on the fast track to Jewish religious leadership when Jesus interrupted all of his ambitious plans on the road to Damascus and called him to preach the gospel to the Gentiles.

Imagine a zealous, Law-abiding Pharisee being commissioned to preach to the Law-less Gentiles. That's what happened to Paul. And as he preached the gospel to them, something amazing happened: they responded. The Gentiles were filled with the Spirit just like the Jews who were coming to faith in Christ. In other words, the Gentile Christian experience paralleled that of the Jewish Christians, except in this regard: the Gentiles were responding to the gospel and being filled with the Spirit *without ever having been circumcised!*

So what was the problem? The Judaizers "knew" God couldn't possibly work that way. After all, ever since the days of Abraham, circumcision had been God's means of defining who was "in" and who was "out." Moses reestablished circumcision as the covenant identity marker for God's people. And for hundreds of years thereafter, Jewish mothers and fathers took their baby boys to the priests for this ritual to be carried out. Even Jesus had been taken to the temple when He was eight days old to be circumcised (Luke 2:21). The Judaizers listed all of these as evidence as to why the Gentiles needed to be circumcised in order to be saved.

At first glance, it might appear that the Judaizers had the scriptural high ground in this debate. The problem, though, was that they completely neglected the voice of the prophets, who had pointed out that there was a *spiritual* circumcision superior to a circumcision of the *flesh* (Jer. 4:4). Not only that, but the Judaizers also ignored the words of Moses himself, the mediator of the Law, who had called Israel to something more than mere religious ritual, when he commanded, "Circumcise your hearts" (Deut. 10:16).

The Judaizers' myopic view of the circumcision tradition blinded them from seeing the Spirit of the Law who was hovering above the letter of the law. As a result, they were convinced God would never fully save the Gentiles without them first embracing the traditional identity markers. Paul, on the other hand, was able to see that if the Gentiles had the Spirit, then they had the only identity marker necessary to belong to God's people. As New Testament scholar Gordon Fee has declared, "The Spirit became the replacement of all the old covenant identity markers!"[6]

"Grace Plus" Versions of the Gospel

Do you know the seven last words of a dying church? "We've never done it that way before." That was the message the Judaizers were shouting to anyone who would listen to them, particularly the leadership of the early church, whom they were convinced needed their instruction.

Let's not be too hard on the Judaizers, though. They're not the only believers in the church's history who have fallen prey to putting God in a very small box. There are Christian traditions today that are just as susceptible to "grace plus" versions of the gospel, where it's assumed (or preached) that we are not *really* saved unless we:

- Get baptized in a specific mode
- Worship God in a particular expression
- Speak in tongues
- Abstain from some version of "The List"
- Home-school our children
- Vote for a certain political party

You can probably think of a few more "grace plus" versions of the gospel.

Eventually, the dividing line between Paul and the Judaizers became so sharply drawn that he felt compelled to go back to Jerusalem to meet with the apostles about this matter. Paul knew he was in the right, but he wanted an endorsement from the other leaders in the church. He needed to make sure the message he had been preaching — that salvation comes by grace alone through faith in Christ — was the same gospel message they were proclaiming.

Paul got what he was looking for, too. The apostles in Jerusalem told him, *You're right on course, Paul. Don't cave into the Judaizers. Stay focused on the message God has called you to preach. The Gentiles don't need to become Jewish to be saved.*

The apostles' response did not come as a surprise to Paul. He already knew the apostle Peter's convictions on this matter. Years earlier, Peter had learned this very same lesson about the Gentiles through his own vision from God (Acts 10). In that epiphany, God called Peter not only to share the good news with the Gentiles, He called Peter to share the table with them as equals.

It cannot be overstated how radical it was for a Jew in the first century to share a meal with a Gentile. It's no wonder Peter was so slow to respond to God on this point; he needed to get the vision three times before he finally accepted it. Like the Judaizers, Peter was certain God could not possibly work this way.

Peter's devotion to the dietary code had become a sacred cow—a religious idol of sorts. Eating kosher had become for Peter and his contemporary Jews a means of justifying their piety to themselves and each other. But as the title of Robert Kriegel's book suggests, "Sacred Cows Make The Best Burgers."[7] God didn't want Peter's sacred cow doing any more mooing. God was doing a new thing, and it meant that keeping the old dietary codes would no longer be the identity marker of His people. Eventually, Peter grasped the lesson God was trying to teach him; he even shared it with the rest of the church's leadership.

Here's the point: Peter had learned directly from God that the gospel was not about saying yes to Jesus and then needing to say yes to circumcision and the dietary laws. The Holy Spirit had made it crystal clear to Peter and the apostles that the truth of the gospel was simply a matter of saying yes to God's grace by way of faith in Jesus. Nothing more and nothing less was required for salvation. And all of the apostles, including Peter, were in agreement about this.

Getting Caught in the Snare of People-Pleasing

This is what makes what Peter did a few years later so tragic. Paul tells the story:

> Before the Judaizers came, Peter used to eat with the Gentiles. But when they arrived, he began to separate himself from the Gentiles because he was afraid of those who belonged to the circumcision group.
>
> —Gal. 2:12

Paul says when push came to shove, Peter caved in to the Judaizers. Why? Because he was afraid of those who belonged to the circumcision group. Peter's decision to draw back from the Gentiles was not based on his convictions changing. It was motivated by his fear of what people would think. He wanted the approval of the highly educated and socially influential Judaizers. And he was willing to compromise the integrity of the gospel to get it.

Let's not be too hard on Peter, though. He certainly didn't have the monopoly on the people-pleasing disease. The majority of the human race can relate to Peter, as the following study, retold by Charles Swindoll, attests.

A few years ago, psychologist Ruth W. Berenda and her associates carried out an interesting experiment with teenagers, designed to show how a person handles group pressure. The plan was simple. They brought groups of ten adolescents into a room for a test. Subsequently, each group of ten was instructed to raise their hands when the teacher pointed to the longest line on three separate charts. What one person in the group did not know was that nine of the others in the room had been instructed ahead of time to vote for the second-longest line. Regardless of the instructions they heard, once they were all together in the group, those nine were not to vote for the longest line, but rather vote for the next-to-the-longest one. Here are the charts as they appeared before each group when the votes were taken.

Chart I	Chart II	Chart III
A ———————	A ———————	A ———————
B —————————	B —————	B ———
C ———	C ———	C —————————

The psychologist's desire was to determine how one person reacted when completely surrounded by a large number of people who obviously stood against what was true.

The experiment began with nine teenagers voting for the wrong line. The tenth person typically would glance around, frown in confusion, and slip his hand up with the group. The instructions were repeated and the next card was raised. Time after time, the tenth person would sit there saying a short line is longer than a long line, simply because he lacked the courage to challenge the group. This remarkable conformity occurred in about 75 percent of the cases, and was true of small children and high school students as well.[8]

My intent is not to equate the apostle Peter with some weak-willed ninth grader. I simply want to highlight that what Proverbs says is true for all of us: "The fear of man will prove to be a snare" (Prov. 29:25). Even Peter was not above getting caught in the snare of people pleasing. And as a result, the early church's leadership found itself at a critical crossroads: *Was anyone going to stand up and speak out against the Judaizers, or was everyone going to sit around and raise their hands for the second-longest line?*

Standing All Alone

Paul knew the very heart of the gospel was at stake. If the Judaizers won this debate, the gospel of grace for which Jesus died would be lost. But what was Paul supposed to do? Just about every other church leader had abandoned the truth and settled for a version of the gospel that was based on keeping the law. All of the key apostles, including Peter and James, had joined the Judaizers' camp.

The real kick in the gut, though, came when Barnabas, Paul's fellow missionary to the Gentiles, also sided with the Judaizers: "The other Jews joined Peter in his hypocrisy, so that even Barnabas was led astray" (Gal. 2:13). Barnabas had been Paul's mentor. Barnabas had been Paul's advocate, standing in the gap for him and helping him get into the ministry when nobody else trusted him. In Paul's early days as a Christian, when he was known simply as a persecutor of the church, it was Barnabas who took a chance on him. It was Barnabas who opened up the ministry doors for Paul to begin preaching the gospel to the Gentiles. And now Barnabas had sided with the Judaizers.

Even Barnabas was led astray.

Imagine the loneliness Paul must have felt when he looked across this theological dividing line and saw on the other side of the fence not only the Judaizers and the apostles, but even Barnabas! "Most of the great souls have been lonely," wrote A.W. Tozer. "Loneliness seems to be the price a saint must pay for his saintliness."[9]

Paul's loneliness was all the more gut wrenching, though, because it was mingled with a sense of betrayal. After all, the other apostles and leaders knew better. God had spoken directly to Peter about this matter three times. But Peter had abandoned the vision. Paul was therefore forced to decide whether he would stand alone for the sake of truth or go with the flow.

There comes a day when every follower of Jesus must decide whether he or she is willing to live out the words from that old hymn, "I Have

Decided to Follow Jesus." How many of us are ready to sing the final verse of that song, which proclaims: "Though none go with me, still I will follow"?

When Abraham Lincoln first penned the Emancipation Proclamation, he polled his presidential cabinet for their votes on the document. The first to vote on the matter of freeing the slaves was the Secretary of State. He stood and uttered his "nay" unmistakably. The Secretary of the Interior stood next. He also voted against the idea. The Treasury Secretary and the rest of the cabinet all followed suit. The president heard each one of the "nays" in turn. Rather than bowing down to political pressure, though, Abraham Lincoln concluded the voting by raising his hand and saying, "The 'ayes' have it."

There comes a day when every follower of Jesus must decide whether he or she is willing to live out the words of that song, "Though none go with me, still I will follow."

There came a day when Edmund G. Ross, a U.S. senator from Kansas, had to make this decision. His story is a reminder that there is a price tag for those willing to swim against the current. Jon Johnston tells Ross's inspiring story:

> I suppose you could call him a "Mr. Nobody." No law bears his name. Not a single list of Senate "greats" mentions his service. Yet when Ross entered the Senate in 1866, he was considered the man to watch. He seemed destined to surpass his colleagues, but he tossed it all away by one courageous act of conscience.

> Let's set the stage. Conflict was dividing our government in the wake of the Civil War. President Andrew Johnson was determined to follow Lincoln's policy of reconciliation toward the defeated South. Congress, however, wanted to rule the downtrodden Confederate states with an iron hand.

> Congress decided to strike first. Shortly after Senator Ross was seated, the Senate introduced impeachment proceedings against the hated President. The radicals calculated that they needed thirty-six votes, and smiled as they concluded that the thirty-sixth was none other than Ross. The new senator listened to the vigilante talk. But to the surprise of many, he declared that the president "deserved as fair a trial

as any accused man has ever had on earth." The word immediately went out that his vote was "shaky."

Ross received an avalanche of anti-Johnson telegrams from every section of the country. Radical senators badgered him to "come to his senses." The fateful day of the vote arrived. The courtroom galleries were packed. Tickets for admission were at an enormous premium.

As a deathlike stillness fell over the Senate chamber, the vote began. By the time they reached Ross, twenty-four "guilties" had been announced. Eleven more were certain. Only Ross's vote was needed to impeach the President. Unable to conceal his emotion, the Chief Justice asked in a trembling voice, "Mr. Senator Ross, how vote you? Is the respondent Andrew Johnson guilty as charged?"

Ross later explained, at that moment, "I looked into my open grave. Friendships, position, fortune, and everything that makes life desirable to an ambitious man were about to be swept away by the breath of my mouth, perhaps forever."

Then, the answer came—unhesitating, unmistakable: "Not guilty!" With that, the trial was over. And the response was as predicted.

A high public official from Kansas wired Ross to say: "Kansas repudiates you as she does all perjurers and skunks." The "open grave" vision had become a reality. Ross' political career was in ruins. Extreme ostracism, and even physical attack awaited his family upon their return home.

One gloomy day Ross turned to his faithful wife and said, "Millions cursing me today will bless me tomorrow…though not but God can know the struggle it has cost me." It was a prophetic declaration.

Twenty years later Congress and the Supreme Court verified the wisdom of his position, by changing the laws related to impeachment.

Ross was appointed Territorial Governor of New Mexico. Then, just prior to his death, he was awarded a special pension by Congress. The press and country took this opportunity to honor his courage, which, they finally concluded, had saved our country from crisis and division.[10]

There comes a day when every follower of Jesus must decide whether he or she is willing to live out the words of that song, "Though none go with me, still I will follow."

That day came many times during Paul's lifetime. But never did it come with greater significance than when he needed to decide how he would respond to his fellow apostles and church leaders who were compromising the gospel's integrity. The stakes could not have been higher for the church. The future of Christianity was hanging in the balance. The key leaders, Peter and James, and even Barnabas had all cast their vote with the Judaizers.

So what were Paul's options at this critical junction? He could have gotten on board with the rest of the apostles and not rocked the boat. Remember, Paul was a Pharisee. He was very comfortable with the Judaizers' way of life. It would have been easy for Paul to justify a compromised position by saying something like, *It's not that big a deal. Gentile Christianity is just becoming a little more kosher. Besides, who am I to stand up against the entire leadership team of the church? James and Peter have already gone along with the Judaizers. Even Barnabas has signed on. Instead of making a federal case out of what is happening here, perhaps I should just tweak my message a bit so that it aligns with what everyone else is saying.*

Paul could have taken the path of least resistance, but he didn't.

One Man with Courage Is a Majority

Paul understood the implications of "tweaking" the gospel message. Besides that, he knew what really had motivated Peter's decision to go along with the Judaizers. People-pleasing, even if masked as diplomacy and peacekeeping, is not an option when it comes to making a decision that compromises Christianity's integrity. This debate was not about the carpet color in the new house-church. It was a theological non-negotiable for which the gospel itself was at stake. This was an issue that warranted, better yet, required, that Paul be willing to stand up and speak the truth, even if it put him at odds with every other church leader around the table. And that is precisely what Paul did:

> When Peter came to Antioch, I opposed him to his face, because he was clearly in the wrong....When I saw that they were not acting in line with the truth of the gospel, I said to Peter in front of them all, "You are a Jew, yet you live like a Gentile and not like a Jew. How is it, then, that you force Gentiles to follow Jewish customs? We...know that a man is not justified by observing the law, but by faith in Jesus Christ."
>
> —Gal. 2:11, 14-15

Paul spoke out against the Judaizers' doctrine. But even more importantly, he stood up to his own peers. He confronted Peter and the other church leaders, who were compromising the truth of the gospel by their complicity with the Judaizers. Paul was willing to stand alone and say what needed to be said. Ultimately, his courageous act was what made the difference in swinging the church leaders back to where they were supposed to be. As Thomas Jefferson once said, "One man with courage is a majority."

The Ripple Effect

Church historians claim that if it weren't for Paul's willingness to stand up to the Judaizers and his fellow church leaders, Christianity would have simply become another religious sect within Judaism. The Judaizers eventually would have won the debate of defining who and how one could be saved. Biblical scholar Gordon Fee argues, "In the end, Christianity wouldn't be here today if Paul hadn't won this battle with the Judaizers, because if you add a plus factor to grace, then the gospel will eventually be null and void. Grace plus 'something' is the absolute death of the Christian faith!"[11]

If Paul hadn't stood up to his peers, then salvation by grace and the freedom for which Christ died would have been lost. In its place, we would have a powerless and perverted form of the gospel, where we keep striving to obtain salvation by trying to obey the Law. And all it would have taken for the early church to go sideways was for Paul to have been a little more attuned to the voices of his neighbors, and a little less attuned to the voice of God.

What if Paul had been more concerned with pleasing the Judaizers and the other apostles than with pleasing Christ? What if Paul had been more concerned about avoiding confrontation with his peers than with standing up for what was right? It's not an exaggeration to say that the ripple effect of that compromise would have been tragic—if not fatal—to the future of Christianity.

But that's not what happened. The truth of the gospel was preserved because one man chose to play for an Audience of One, because one man was willing to follow God even if that put him at odds with his peers, because one man set his heart on pleasing Christ more than on pleasing people, because one man tuned his ears to the voice of God rather than to the voices of his neighbors.

Paul played for an Audience of One.

What About Us?

Imagine if Christ's church were filled with people willing to follow in the apostle Paul's footsteps, willing to live with this same conviction about playing for an Audience of One, willing to relinquish all people-pleasing tendencies, and willing to focus all of our energy on seeking to please God.

Deep down, isn't this the way you want to live?

Even as I write these words, I'm reminded of a conversation with a woman who has been part of our church for twenty years. After being inspired by how Paul's example of playing for an Audience of One preserved the gospel, Jana decided she was fed up living with her ear to the rail of public opinion. She acknowledged how inclined she was to people-please whenever she entered into conversations with her fellow Christians, how ensnared she was by the fear of what others thought of her whenever she needed to make a difficult decision that might diminish her popularity, and how consumed she was with gaining people's accolades when she sang in church. Toward the end of our conversation, Jana wept quietly as she asked a question that served more as a confession than something requiring a response: "Why is it so important to me that I gain people's approval?"

God is honoring Jana's confession. Her brokenness led her to make a commitment to live for God's approval alone. She's on the path of playing for an Audience of One, and it's beginning to bear fruit in her life. The final line of a recent letter I received from her read, "I think I am finally learning a little bit about what it means to play for an Audience of One."

Pastors struggle with this, too. Recently, a ministry leader shared with me the journey of his struggle to stay true to what he knows God has called him to do. This pastor oversees worship and music at his church. In a moment of transparency, he admitted, "There was a season in my ministry when I was constantly attending worship committee meetings—*the kind that meet only in my head.*"

He described how when Sunday mornings rolled around, there would be certain people in the congregation who would express their disappointment, frustration, and even anger regarding his musical style and selection. As a result, he had a habit of meeting with them (in his mind) and letting their opinions and criticisms dictate the direction of each Sunday's worship service. The antidote to these "mental worship committee meetings," he said, was to practice tuning his ears to hear God's still, small voice. The result of this "tuning" ritual has been a life marked with a greater sense of peace and freedom, and a ministry that has God's stamp of approval on it.

The same thing can happen for you.

The situations in which you and I are tempted to go along with the crowd might not be as historically significant as they were for Paul, Luther, or Lincoln. But that doesn't mean that the stakes aren't still high. The consequences of living for your peers' approval are steep. The price you pay when you give in to the fear of people is higher than you might think. On the other hand, there is a huge upside when even *one* person gives him or herself entirely to playing for an Audience of One. This is the subject matter of the rest of the book. But you can't move on from here until you first answer Paul's Galatians 1:10 question for yourself: *Am I now trying to win the approval of men, or of God?*

Drawing a line in the sand

Are you ready to embark on a journey where playing for an Audience of One truly begins to define your life? Unless you give the consent of your will, this journey will be merely informative. Information is good, but it won't lead to transformation unless your will is engaged. As A.W. Tozer wrote:

> In speaking thus, I have one fear: that I may convince the mind before God can win the heart. For this God-above-all position is one not easy to take. The mind may approve it while not having the consent of the will to put it into effect. While the imagination races ahead to honor God, the will may lag behind and the man must make the decision before the heart can know any real satisfaction. God wants the whole person and He will not rest till He gets us in entirety.[12]

Are you ready to make your decision to play for an Audience of One? Doing so doesn't mean it will happen overnight, but it won't ever happen until your will is fully engaged.

Does your mind have the consent of your will? If so, then say this prayer as a way of committing yourself to the journey of learning to play for an Audience of One. But be careful what you pray for; God loves to answer this kind of prayer!

Prayer of a God-pleaser

> O God, nothing of earth's treasures shall seem dear unto me if only Thou are glorified in my life....I am determined that Thou shalt be above all, though I must stand deserted and alone in the midst of the earth....I shall keep my vow made this day before Thee. Be Thou exalted over my reputation. Make me ambitious to please Thee even if as a result I must sink into obscurity and my name be forgotten as a dream. Rise, O Lord, into Thy proper place of honor, above my ambitions, above my likes and dislikes, above my family, my health, and even my life itself. Let me sink that Thou mayest rise above. Ride forth upon me as Thou didst ride into Jerusalem mounted upon the humble little beast, a colt, the foal of a donkey, and let me hear the children cry to Thee, "Hosanna in the highest!" Amen.[13]

—A.W. Tozer

Going Deeper

1. Even if the stakes surrounding your stands for truth aren't as high as they were for Paul, they're probably higher than you think. For instance:

   • Parents: Is the discomfort you feel when your kids are angry with you so great that you compromise what needs to be said or done in order to keep their affections? Are you willing to set your friendship with them aside at those points when disciplining them is required?

   • Husband/Wife: Is the pain you feel in the face of your spouse's disapproval so overwhelming that you compromise what needs to be said or done in order to keep the peace, even when you know you should speak up?

   • Peer Relationships: Do you go along with your friends and peers at work, school, or church even when you know in your gut that what they're saying or doing is not pleasing to God, because the discomfort you would feel if you were all alone seems too overwhelming not to join them?

2. If you're part of a church, encourage your pastors and leaders to play for an Audience of One. You may not realize how susceptible leaders are to "listening to the voice of their neighbors." Write them or let them know you are praying for them in this matter. In doing so, you will communicate your encouragement to them. In addition, you will remind them of the importance of their making the right decisions even when they may be unpopular.

3. Don't let this story be reduced to a license for your becoming the church watchdog over matters of relative insignificance. Paul stood up against something that was perverting the very nature of the gospel. Not every issue requires the same kind of passionate refusal to compromise. Pray for the discernment to know the difference.

4. If you find yourself in a church where the gospel's integrity really is being compromised, pray for the courage and wisdom to communicate what needs to be said. But check your motives before you

do anything. One rule of thumb for confrontation is that you have truly grieved and wept for those people who are in the wrong before you seek to challenge or correct them.

Chapter 3

THE DISCIPLE JESUS LOVED

When you're in your twenties,
you live to please other people.
When you're in your thirties,
you're tired of trying to please others,
and you get miffed with them for making you worry about it.
When you're in your forties,
you realize nobody was thinking about you
in the first place.[14]

WHEN INTRODUCING YOURSELF to someone, what do you say? For instance if you have fifteen seconds to identify who you are, how do you talk about yourself? Go ahead and pretend to introduce yourself to someone who doesn't know anything about you. Really. I'm listening.

If you're anything like me, you probably respond by talking about what you *do*. Typically, this is what happens: we provide a thumbnail sketch of our job, highlight the roles we play in our family, and perhaps mention a few of our other responsibilities. The specifics might vary from person to person, but most of us respond to this question of who we are by giving some form of a verbal résumé.

There is a stereotype that men are the ones who most deeply feel this connection between who they *are* and what they *do*. Men are not the only ones who think about themselves in terms of résumés and job titles, though. Women are inclined to do the same thing. One stay-at-home mom tells the story of how she decided to start identifying herself:

> Upon picking up my children at school, another mom I knew well rushed up to me, fuming with indignation. "Do you know what people think you and I are?"
>
> My friend had just returned from renewing her driver's license. Asked by the county clerk to state her occupation, she had hesitated, uncertain how to classify herself.
>
> The clerk had asked her the question, "Do you have a job, or are you *just a…?*"
>
> "Of course I have a job," my friend had snapped. "I'm a mother!"
>
> "We don't list 'mother' as an occupation," the clerk had said emphatically. My friend was outraged as she replayed the offense for me.
>
> I forgot all about my friend's story until one day I found myself in the same situation, this time at our own town hall. The clerk behind the counter was obviously a career woman, poised, efficient, and the possessor of a high and lofty-sounding title like "Official Interrogator" or "Town Registrar."
>
> "And what is your occupation?" she asked me.
>
> What made me respond the way I did, I don't know. The words just popped out: "I'm a research associate in the field of child development and human relations."
>
> The clerk paused, her ballpoint pen frozen in midair. She looked up as though she had not heard right. I repeated the title slowly, emphasizing the most significant words: "I'm a *research* associate in the field of child *development* and human *relations.*"
>
> Then I stared with wonder as my pronouncement was written in bold, black ink on the official questionnaire.

"Might I ask," said the clerk with new interest, "just what you do in your field?"

Calmly, without any trace of fluster in my voice, I heard myself reply, "I have a continuing program of research (what mother doesn't) in the laboratory and in the field (normally I would have said indoors and out). I'm working for my master's (basically, the whole family) and already I have four credits (all daughters). Of course, the job is one of the most demanding in the humanities (any mother care to disagree?) and I often work fourteen hours a day (twenty-four is more like it). The job is more challenging than most run-of-the-mill careers but the rewards come in terms of personal satisfaction rather than just money."

There was an increasing note of respect in the clerk's voice as she completed the form, stood up, and personally ushered me to the door.

As I drove into my driveway at home, buoyed by my glamorous new career, I was greeted by my lab assistants—ages thirteen, seven, and three. Upstairs, I could hear my new experimental model (six months old) in the child development program, testing out a new vocal pattern. I felt triumphant! I had gone on the official records that day as more than *just a mom*. Motherhood: what a glorious career—especially when there's a title on the door![15]

It's natural to take pride in what you do. After all, what you do has eternal significance and is deeply connected to who you are. The inclination to link 'who you are' with 'what you do' should not come as a surprise. It was hard-wired into us at creation. God's first command to Adam was to *do* something: "Take care of the Garden" (Gen. 2:15, paraphrased).

But "doing" was never intended to be the whole story of who we are. God did not create us solely to do things—as important as those things are that He asks us to do. We are human *beings*, not human *doings*.

Social etiquette being what it is, most people expect to hear some form of a verbal résumé greeting during those fifteen seconds when you introduce yourself. I'm not so much taking issue with the social formalities that influence what we say during an introduction. Of greater concern is that so many of us actually think about who we are in terms of our verbal résumé.

Playing for an Audience of One begins not with doing anything for God, but in viewing yourself the way He sees you—regardless of what anyone else thinks about your résumé. How do you do this? I don't believe there is anybody better suited to be our teacher on this topic than John, the author of the fourth gospel.

John's Résumé

How did John view himself? Let me ask the question this way: If John had been asked to identify himself in fifteen seconds or less, what would he have said? Well, here's what he could have said about himself. It's probably what I would have said about him if I were introducing him: *John was one of the twelve apostles. He was a key leader in the church. He was an evangelist. He became the pastor and teacher of the highly influential church at Ephesus. Finally, he authored five books in the New Testament, penning the Gospel that bears his name—1, 2, and 3 John—and the book of Revelation.*

Apostle. Leader. Evangelist. Pastor. Teacher. Author. That is quite an impressive résumé, don't you think?

But here's the thing about John: he never identified himself with any of these titles. He did identify himself throughout his gospel account—five times, in fact. He referred to himself the same way every time; in a way that reveals how he truly perceived himself. And John didn't need fifteen seconds to identify who he was. He only needed five words. The way he identified himself throughout his gospel account was so simple, and yet so profound: he was *the disciple whom Jesus loved.*[16]

At first glance, you might be tempted to think John was a bit arrogant for proclaiming himself *the* disciple Jesus loved—as though he had the monopoly on Jesus' love. After all, Jesus loved the other disciples, too. John wasn't being arrogant or exclusive, though. In fact, it was John, more than any other gospel writer, who wrote the most about Jesus' love for the whole world. So how was it that John felt justified portraying himself as the disciple Jesus loved?

The more time I spend with John and his writings, the more certain I am that it was not elitism that was moving him to pen those words about himself. Rather, it was a deep, God-given conviction about who he was. If the Gospel of John is inspired, then it follows that the way John identified himself is also inspired—not because Jesus loved him more than He loved the other disciples, but because God intended that we, who would read these words, learn something from the way John viewed himself.

John knew two things about himself with unshakable certainty:

1. Jesus called him to be His *disciple*.
2. Jesus *loved* him passionately.

Over time, these two convictions became forged into one ultimate identity statement for John: he was the disciple Jesus loved.[17]

Exchanging Ambition for Affection

What's so striking about John's identity statement is this was the same John Jesus had nicknamed "son of thunder" — the one who had, earlier in his life, jockeyed for the position of sitting at Jesus' right or left hand of power. I recently saw a poster depicting a lightning-filled sky with a caption at the bottom that read, "Power corrupts, and absolute power corrupts absolutely…but it rocks absolutely, too!"[18] That was the motto of the old John, the power hungry opportunist, who was always looking to get ahead in Jesus' kingdom administration. But somewhere along the journey, John willingly abandoned his ambitious pursuit of power and prestige in exchange for an identity based on Christ's affection.

Titles, authority, and every other status symbol—all of that became worthless to John compared to an identity defined by the fact that Jesus was head over heels in love with him. Brennan Manning makes the case that coming to the realization that God is "head over heels in love with you" is at the core of our ability to grow spiritually. He writes that if in our hearts we are still tainted by the lie that we can do something to make God love us more than He already does, we are rejecting the message of the Cross.[19]

Manning seeks to open our eyes to the reality that God is our Abba, our Daddy, whose love and affection for us can actually transform the way we view ourselves. By way of illustration, he tells the story of a priest from Detroit, named Edward Farrell, who went on a two-week summer vacation to Ireland to celebrate the eightieth birthday of his one living uncle. It was the priest who ended up being the student in a Theology 101 course taught by his Uncle Seamus.

> On the great day, the priest and his uncle got up before dawn and dressed in silence. They took a walk along the shores of Lake Killarney and stopped to watch the sunrise. Standing side by side with not a word exchanged and staring straight at the rising sun, suddenly the uncle turned and went skipping down the road. He was radiant, beaming, smiling from ear to ear.
>
> His nephew said, "Uncle Seamus, you really look happy."
>
> "I am, lad."
>
> "Want to tell me why?"
>
> His 80 year-old uncle replied, "Yes, you see, my Abba is very fond of me."[20]

How might I view myself if I knew God was very fond of me? Not just that God loves me because He is doctrinally obligated to love me, but because He is *fond* of me? It's one thing to believe God so loves the world. It's another to live with the deep conviction that God so loves *me*.

Karl Barth arguably was the greatest theologian of the twentieth century. His twelve-volume *Church Dogmatics* consists of over ten thousand pages of systematic theology. Toward the end of his life, Barth made a tour of the United States, where he had the opportunity to speak at several of our nation's top universities. During a question and answer time following one of his lectures, a student posed what seemed an impossible question to answer.

"Dr. Barth, you have written extensively on every aspect of theology and church history. I'm wondering if you could sum it all up in a short sentence or two."

The room fell silent. Dr. Barth just stood there for a moment, carefully considering how to respond. Some of the professors and students who were there clearly began to feel awkward that such a trifling question would be asked of such a brilliant scholar.

Finally, Karl Barth turned toward the student and succinctly replied, "Jesus loves me, this I know, for the Bible tells me so."

The apostle John knew a lot about Jesus, too. He had spent over three years with Him. He was part of the inner circle of disciples who received insider information about Jesus' mission, and front-row seats to miracles and mountaintop experiences. John could have written his own twelve-volume work about Jesus. In fact, John said there was so much that could be said about Jesus that the world itself wasn't big enough to contain all of the books that could be written (John 21:25). However, at the end of the day, John would have echoed Barth's response had someone asked him the same question. It was John's simple realization that Jesus was head over heels in love with him that served as the bottom line for everything he knew about God. His knowledge of that love so captured him that it completely shaped the way he viewed God and, therefore, the way he viewed himself.

John had an impressive sounding résumé: apostle, evangelist, pastor, leader, teacher, and author. But all of that paled in comparison to how John ultimately viewed himself: as the disciple Jesus loved. Have you ever noticed how much John wrote about God's love? Think about it:

"For God so loved the world."

—John 3:16

"How great is the love the Father has lavished on us."

—1 John 3:1

"God is love!"

—1 John 4:8

People who have been gripped by the realization of God's love cannot help but share that love with others. It just pours out of them. They talk about it. They write about it. They live it. That's what happened to John after his eyes were opened to the depth and breadth of Jesus' love for him. This "son of thunder," who earlier in his life had requested Jesus call down fire from heaven to torch the unresponsive Samaritans (Luke 9:54), became the disciple Jesus loves. And from that point on, John's life and letters just drip with this love.

A similar thing happened to Thomas Aquinas, arguably the greatest Catholic theologian ever, and certainly one of the most prolific writers in church history.

> Toward the end of his life, Aquinas suddenly stopped writing. When his secretary complained that his work was unfinished, Thomas replied, "Brother Reginald, when I was at prayer a few months ago, I experienced something of the reality of Jesus Christ. That day, I lost all appetite for writing. In fact, all I have ever written about Christ seems now to me to be like straw."[21]

Thomas Aquinas abandoned his ambition to be the greatest theologian and author in church history. He relinquished that identity marker in exchange for one that was founded upon Jesus' affection. Aquinas became more attuned to the voice of God than the voices of those around him who were telling him who he was supposed to be and what he was supposed to do.

Should We Do Less?

I probably need to make a disclaimer at this point: just because you begin to view yourself as a disciple Jesus loves does not necessarily mean you will do less for God. Doing less is not the point. The point is that whatever you do for God should flow out of an identity rooted in Christ's love. Otherwise, you will default to a life of frantic striving, where you're constantly seeking to appease God, justify yourself or impress others with what you're doing. In doing so, you'll find yourself running on a self-justification treadmill that only leads to spiritual exhaustion. And the only way to jump off the treadmill is to stop believing Satan's lie about who you are. As Robert McGee writes:

Basing our self-worth on what we believe others think of us causes us to become addicted to their approval. Turning to others for what only God can provide is a direct result of our acceptance of Satan's lie: Self Worth = Performance + Others' Opinions[22]

The Path to Rest and Peace: Meekness

Playing for an Audience of One begins with learning to mute the world's voices, which beckon for your attention. These voices lie to you about who you are. What you really need is a healthy indifference to the world's opinions of you. In a word, you need meekness:

> The meek man knows well that the world will never see him as God sees him and he has stopped caring. He rests perfectly content to allow God to place His own values. He will be patient to wait for the day when everything will get its own price tag and real worth will come into its own.[23]

Not only is this the right way to view yourself, Thomas a Kempis reminds us that meekness is also the path to rest and peace. Rest and peace are something which most of us would enjoy having more of, but pride blocks the way. Meekness is the gift from Jesus that frees us from our pride: "The proud man and the covetous man never have rest; but the meek man and the poor in spirit live in great abundance of rest and peace."[24]

The first and foremost question you must ask yourself, then, is: *Do you want this rest and peace badly enough to jump off the treadmill and learn meekness?*

Feedback Is the Breakfast of Champions!

For me, learning meekness has moved to the front burner of my life since becoming a pastor. I share from my own journey at this point, not because I have the identity issue all figured out, nor because I think being a pastor makes this challenge any more difficult than for other followers of Jesus. I simply want to paint a picture of how meekness can be pursued in real life.

As a pastor, there are times when I am on the receiving end of "constructive criticism." Much of the critique I've received over the years has been very helpful in making my character, leadership, and the overall ministry of our church more pleasing to God. I don't pretend to be without my shortcomings. I have blind spots. As painful as it can be to hear the criticism, I've come to accept that there are times when I need the perspective and correction of others.

When I was finally willing to acknowledge this, I committed Psalm 141:5 to memory. I learned to rehearse it (in my mind) when people would report to me their constructive criticisms. As I listened to the critiques, the Spirit would help me recite this verse to myself: "Let a righteous man strike me—it is a kindness; let him rebuke me—it is oil to my head. My head will not refuse it."

One of my mantras in life is: "Feedback is the breakfast of champions!" I have this slogan written in the margin of my Bible next to Psalm 141:5. I've realized if I want to grow, I need to be able to digest critique and criticism for its full nourishment potential. It still doesn't come naturally to me, but at those points when I've been mature enough to swallow my pride and let go of my tendency to get defensive, mining criticism for nuggets of truth has proven to be invaluable. So on the one hand, I am thankful for these comments.

On the other hand, in terms of what these comments can do to my self-esteem, I'll be honest. It's not pleasant to hear things from people that reinforce the truth that I am far from perfect. I certainly know I'm not perfect, but it's not my goal to prove to the rest of the world how far from perfect I really am! Criticism has become a testing ground for where my identity lies. In other words, it forces me to wrestle with the question: *How will I view myself when other people discover and then call out my shortcomings?*

When People Take My Picture Out of Their Wallets

You know the saying: *Better to be thought a fool than to open your mouth and prove it.* Well, being a pastor means I frequently am opening my mouth. So it's no wonder I have been thought a fool from time to time. Even more often, opening my mouth has served to catalyze disagreements, instigate conflict, and, at times, give voice to decisions that disappoint people. These situations have also become opportunities for me to demonstrate (to myself and others) where my true identity lies. In other words: *How will I view myself when my public approval rating takes a hit?*

Here's the lesson that I'm learning: It's not the end of the world when people take my picture out of their wallets.

Time for confession: There have been good reasons why some people have canceled their memberships to my fan club. Perhaps I was insensitive in the way I spoke to them, or maybe I made a shortsighted decision that negatively impacted them or the ministry area where they served. Having my identity rooted in Christ does not give me license to be a jerk or an excuse to make thoughtless decisions. But there have been other times when people have taken my picture out of their wallets because I said something I knew God wanted me to say and the person just didn't want to hear it, because I faithfully preached a Scripture and it ruffled feathers, or because I made a tough call (that I knew needed to be made) and it put me at odds with someone who strongly disagreed with that decision.

I'm learning that sometimes this is just what happens when I seek to please God. This can be one of the results when my goal in life is not to make sure everyone likes me. Don't get me wrong, I enjoy it when people like and appreciate me. It's not my purpose in life to tick off people. However, I'm learning that it's not the end of the world if and when that happens.

I cannot say passionately enough how critical it is to learn this lesson if you are going to play for an Audience of One. For some of us, the prospect of people being mad at us or disappointed in us is almost more than we can bear. If this is the case for you, it may be a sign that you have some identity work to do.

Many of us need to replace Satan's equation: *Who I am = my performance + other people's opinions of me* with the equation Jesus gives: *Who I am = Whose I am.*

When my mind is focused on this equation, then even in those situations where my public approval rating dips, I know my true identity: I am a disciple Jesus loves. I am not the product of my less than stellar leadership decisions, a reflection of my résumé of failures, or an extension of people's disapproval and disappointment. I am a disciple Jesus loves, and the reminder of my true identity lifts me up and brings me back to a proper, biblical perspective of who and Whose I am.

Don't Read Your Own Press

Just as dangerous to my true identity are those times when I think about the applause and accolades I get from people. I'm not talking about notes of thanks or simple words of encouragement. I'm referring to those times when people put me on a pedestal; those times when someone, for whatever reason, thinks I am the greatest thing since sliced bread and then tells me so; those times when I discover someone out there is carrying an 8x10 picture of me around in his or her wallet!

Jesus said, "Woe to you when all men speak well of you" (Luke 6:26). Or, as a friend of mine likes to say, "Beware when people start drinking your bathwater!" In those moments when my public approval rating is soaring, I've learned to be very intentional about not reading my own press. It's amazing how quickly I can default to letting other people's glowing (sometimes gushing) reviews of me color my thinking about myself. There's a fine line between accepting someone's appreciation and indulging in grandiosity. Admiration can be just as much a snare to my view of who I am as those occasions when I am questioned and criticized.

Applause has this insidious propensity for distracting and deceiving us about who we really are. Spiritual leaders are not immune from the temptation to let others' approval shore up the way we view ourselves. Nobody is immune. That's why settling the identity issue is so critical. When I find myself slipping into a posture where my ego is allowing people's applause to influence the way I view myself, the reminder that I am a disciple Jesus loves appropriately humbles me, and brings me back to a proper, biblical perspective of who and Whose I am.

Don't Settle for a Pseudo-Identity

Any identity based on a résumé of accomplishments (or the lack thereof) is a pseudo-identity. Unfortunately, many of us often slip into this kind of thinking without even trying. Why are we so prone to view ourselves this way? Henri Nouwen sums up the real issue with which we all struggle. He writes:

> At issue here is the question: "To whom do I belong? To God or to the world?" Many of my daily preoccupations suggest that I belong more to the world than to God. A little criticism makes me angry, and a little rejection makes me depressed. A little praise raises my spirits, and a little success excites me....I am like a small boat on the ocean, completely at the mercy of its waves.[25]

Although I'm striving to play for an Audience of One, Nouwen's confession still describes me more than I'd like to admit. Given the title of this book, you might think I no longer care what people think. Unfortunately, even as I've been writing, I've found myself distracted by the hope that you, the reader, would think my words wise and profound. From there I'm daydreaming about how significant this book could be in the lives of fellow believers, and therefore, how significant it would make me look. It's not pure ego driving me. Much of my ambition flows out of a true desire to bring God glory and do what I know He has called me to do. But there is a part of me that still craves after the pseudo-identity markers of résumé and reputation.

Brennan Manning shares his confession on this matter:

> For many years I hid from my true self through my performance in ministry. I constructed an identity through sermons, books, and storytelling. I rationalized that if the majority of Christians thought well of me, there was nothing wrong with me. The more I invested in ministerial success, the more real the impostor became.[26]

Many of us could make the same confession, simply by replacing Manning's words, "my performance in ministry" with "my performance in _____."

Even those who have been deemed "successful" will face the temptation to continue pressing on for more significant sounding pseudo-identity markers. Christina was valedictorian in her class of over four hundred students, a leader in her youth group, and well respected among her peers. And yet she still battled with what people thought about her. She wrote me this e-mail following our spiritual renewal retreat, where a group of us spent the weekend doing business with God about this matter of how we view ourselves:

> I'm a perfectionist. I know that about myself. But I've realized that much of my perfectionism is done, in part, because I love getting approval from people. Who doesn't? Unfortunately, because of how badly I've wanted people to like me, I found myself changing who I am to fit what I think they want me to be—to the point where I didn't know who I was anymore. My mood from day to day would depend on how my friends reacted to me.
>
> But I'm discovering that I'm bound to be disappointed when I look to others for my sense of self-worth. I'm realizing how destructive being addicted to their approval can be.
>
> I'm still struggling with it and I have a feeling that I will for a while, but I have hope now. I've been looking to God for approval and trying not to care so much about what others think about me. It's still hard, and some days are kind of depressing, but I'm learning to carry my frustrations and disappointment to God and let Him remind me who I really am.

The Tyranny of the Treadmill

Until you step off the résumé and reputation treadmill, you will continually be plagued by the kind of questions that reinforce Satan's lie about who you are:

- Employees in the workforce will wonder: "Have I climbed high enough up the job ladder so that I feel okay when I respond to the question of what I do?"
- Stay-at-home moms will wrestle with the question: "Is what I'm doing significant or should I be pursuing a career out there in the 'real' world?"
- Moms who work outside the home will be haunted by comparison-trap questions such as: "What will the 'stay-at-home moms' think about me because I work outside the home?"

- Senior citizens will despair when they are unable to do the work for God that they used to do. I've seen how elderly people's inability to serve Christ in the same way as in the early years of their spiritual journey frequently leads them to ask questions such as: "Does God still love me?" and "Am I still saved?"
- Students wonder: "Will I make the grade?" and "What will happen to me if I don't make it into that circle of friends?"

The list could go on and on. All of us are tempted to some degree to ask ourselves these kinds of questions. But these are the wrong questions to be asking, because they draw us away from the reality of our identity in Christ, and subtly deceive us into chasing after a pseudo-identity based on reputation and success.

The price tag for this kind of life is restlessness, discontentment, and fatigue. Basing your identity on success and public approval is like having to run a marathon, and then when it's over running another one, and then another one, and then another one. Richard Swenson writes about why so many of us are so physically and emotionally tired:

> Preoccupation with success deprives us of rest—always climb a little higher and get a little more. We worry about our image and our reputation until we have no rest.[27]

True Rest

Only an identity completely wrapped up in Jesus will bring true rest. What Augustine said 1,600 years ago is as true today as it was then: "Our hearts are restless until they find their rest in Thee."

Finding complete rest in Christ does not usually happen when you first trust Him for the forgiveness of sins. Forgiveness is but the initial step in what God wants to do in and for you. Most of us struggle to experience the full rest that Christ offers because we can't yet hear His voice over the roar of the voices (our own included) yelling at us to keep running on the treadmill. Jesus wants to do more than simply free you from the consequences of your sin. He wants to free you from Satan's lie about how you view yourself. He wants to free you from running after an identity that is based on résumé and reputation. He wants to free you to be at rest with who you were created to be: a disciple Jesus loves.

Few human beings have experienced and modeled this kind of rest as authentically as Brother Dominique. I've shared his story with so many people in my church that some consider Dominique an honorary member of our fellowship. Stephen, a janitor at a local high school in our community, even photocopied the following story about Dominique, and hung it up in his custodial closet. He did so to remind himself of who and Whose he really is.

> Brother Dominique learned at age fifty-four that he was dying of inoperable cancer. With the community's permission, he moved to a poor neighborhood in Paris and took a job as night watchman at a factory. Returning home every morning at eight A.M., he would go directly to a little park across the street from where he lived and sit down on a wooden bench. Hanging around the park were marginal people, drifters, winos, "has-beens," dirty old men who ogled the girls passing by.

> Dominique never criticized, scolded, or reprimanded them. He laughed, told stories, shared his candy, and accepted them just as they were. From living so long out of the inner sanctuary, he gave off a peace, a serene sense of self-possession and a hospitality of heart that caused cynical young men and defeated old men to gravitate toward him like bacon toward eggs. His simple witness lay in accepting others as they were without questions and allowing them to make themselves at home in his heart. Dominique was the most nonjudgmental person I have ever known. He loved with the heart of Jesus Christ.

> One day, when the ragtag group of rejects asked him to talk about himself, Dominique gave them a thumbnail description of his life. Then he told them with quiet conviction that God loved them tenderly and stubbornly, that Jesus had come for rejects and outcasts just like themselves. His witness was credible because the Word was enfleshed on his bones. Later one old-timer said, "The dirty jokes, vulgar language, and leering at girls just stopped."

One morning Dominique failed to appear on his park bench. The men grew concerned. A few hours later, he was found dead on the floor of his cold-water flat. He died in the obscurity of a Parisian slum.

Dominique Voillaume never tried to impress anybody, never wondered if his life was useful or his witness meaningful. He never felt he had to do something great for God. He did keep a journal. It was found shortly after his death in the drawer of the nightstand by his bed. His last entry is one of the most astonishing things I have every read: "All that is not the love of God has no meaning for me. I can truthfully say that I have no interest in anything but the love of God, which is in Christ Jesus. If God wants it to, my life will be useful through my word and witness. If He wants it to, my life will bear fruit through my prayers and sacrifices. But the usefulness of my life is His concern, not mine. It would be indecent of me to worry about that."[28]

Imagine living with this kind of freedom from the tyranny of résumé and reputation. Jesus wants this for you even more than you want it for yourself. But it won't happen until you step off the treadmill and accept the truth of who and Whose you are, until you exchange an identity that is founded on ambition for one that is based on Christ's affection, and until you, like John, learn to identify yourself simply as a disciple Jesus loves.

Prayer of a Disciple Jesus Loves

Father, help me get to the place where I can truly say I have no interest in being identified by anything other than Your love. If You want it to, my life will be useful through what I say or what I do. But the usefulness of my life is up to You, not me. Help me not to worry about that.

—Brother Dominique (paraphrase)

Going Deeper

1. Write out the parts of your "résumé" that keep you on the pseudo-identity treadmill. Prayerfully exchange your ambitions for an identity based on Christ's affection.
2. Spend some time asking God to give you an identity statement. For example: "disciple Jesus loves," "the beloved," "man of God," "child of the King," or something else you sense God calling you when you're closest to Him.
3. Memorize a Scripture that reinforces the truth of who and Whose you really are. Practice reciting it during moments when you are tempted to default to old ways of thinking about yourself.
4. Read anything by Brennan Manning, but especially *Abba's Child* or *Ragamuffin Gospel*.

Chapter 4

WHAT'S IN YOUR HAND?

"I am a bow in your hands, Lord.
Draw me, lest I rot.
Do not overdraw me, Lord. I shall break.
Overdraw me, Lord, and who cares if I break."[29]
—Nikos Kazantzakis

REMEMBER THE TELEVISION program "MacGyver"? The show played during the late eighties, and featured secret agent, Angus "Mac" MacGyver, whose claim to fame was that he refused to carry a gun. Instead of packing a firearm, he found a way to do the job by relying on his vast scientific knowledge and unparalleled resourcefulness. It was remarkable how many different ways he got himself out of a jam:

- He stopped an acid leak with a chocolate candy bar.
- He replaced a complicated electrode with a nail, wire, and some jumper cables.
- He created a small explosive using an ordinary stick of gum.
- He fixed a computer with a hairpin and a piece of duct tape.

All MacGyver needed was an ordinary, everyday item at his disposal, and he was impossible to stop. There was no obstacle he couldn't overcome, no disaster he couldn't curtail. He could thwart the bad guys and bring about world peace with a paperclip! As long as MacGyver could get his hands on something—it could be anything—it was just a matter of time before he accomplished the mission.

If only our hands had this Midas touch. Imagine what we could do for God! Unfortunately, most of us feel like we're all thumbs when it comes to accomplishing anything for God's kingdom.

It's true that what you do does not define who you are, but once you know who you are, you are called to do something. Deep down we all want our lives to count. That's how God designed us. Even those who don't believe in God or an afterlife still want their lives to contribute to some sort of legacy after they're gone. How much more for us who believe God's mission is to build a kingdom that will last forever?

We know our lives have the potential to impact eternity. But if you're honest with yourself, don't you secretly wonder whether you have what it takes to do anything of eternal significance?

Take a couple of minutes to reflect on the question: *Is my life, in some meaningful way, serving to fulfill God's mission in the world?*

Looks Can Be Deceiving

One of the most common pitfalls that trip us up as Christians is our definition of "meaningful." Many of us have a skewed idea about what constitutes real significance in the kingdom. We're tempted to believe that only those with high profile, upfront leadership gifts can do anything really meaningful to fulfill God's mission in the world. Those of us with ordinary, seemingly unimpressive gifts have a tendency to view ourselves as second-string Christians. We then become content to stand on the sidelines and cheer on the "star players" of God's team.

When your life's goal becomes to play for an Audience of One, standing on the sidelines is no longer an option. God wants everyone in the game—no matter how ordinary you think your gifts might be, or how insecure you feel about using them. Besides, you should be wary of trying to measure the meaningfulness of your service in terms of mere externals. It's easy to fall prey to comparing what you're doing for God with what others are doing. Kingdom-significance, though, is not measured by the apparent size of the gift used *for* God, but by the degree to which that gift has been surrendered *to* God. Playing for an Audience of One is about recognizing what little you bring to the table, but then committing it to God. From there, it's up to God to do what He wants with it.

Brother Lawrence referred to himself as "the lord of all pots and pans" because he never climbed any higher up the job ladder than cook and bottle washer. Yet the impact of his life on God's kingdom was incalculable because the apparent insignificance of his kitchen duties didn't stop him from fully surrendering them to God. "It is not necessary to have great things to do. I turn my little omelets in the pan for the love of God," he said.[30]

Remember Brother Dominique's words: "The usefulness of my life is His concern, not mine. It would be indecent of me to worry about that." Ironically, Brother Lawrence and Brother Dominique were both used in extremely meaningful ways to advance God's kingdom, despite the fact that their respective ministry environments (the kitchen and the street corner) appeared to be insignificant.

Looks can be deceiving.

It's Not Too Late

Reflecting on this question of what we are doing for God can be gut wrenching—especially for those of us who know we've squandered too many years on trivial pursuits. If that is where you are today, though, don't despair. It's not too late for your life to count for the kingdom. After all, Moses was eighty years old, living in the middle of the desert, and taking care of someone else's flock of sheep when God finally got his attention. So when I begin to doubt myself and question the impact my life can have on this world, I look to an old desert shepherd for inspiration and perspective.

Clenched Fists

Moses was born into a Hebrew family in the land of Egypt, where his people had been enslaved for nearly four hundred years. The number of Hebrew slaves had grown so rapidly that Pharaoh, fearing a revolt, mandated that every one of their baby boys be killed at birth. When

Moses was born, though, his mother devised a courageous, Pharaoh-defying, God-honoring plan: she placed her baby in a basket along the bank of the Nile River, and then prayed for a miracle. She got it.

Pharaoh's daughter "just happened to be" bathing in the Nile River, and when she saw the basket lying in the reeds, she sent one of her attendants to retrieve it. In that tiny floating ark she discovered baby Moses. Pharaoh's daughter felt sorry for the baby, so she brought him into the palace, where he was raised with all of the privileges of a royal upbringing.

But when Moses grew up, He came into contact with the harsh reality of slavery from which he had been insulated all of his life. He wasn't prepared for what he saw:

> One day, after Moses had grown up, he went out to where his own people were and watched them at their hard labor. He saw an Egyptian beating a Hebrew, one of his own people.
>
> —Ex. 2:11

Despite the fact that Moses had been raised with a silver spoon in his mouth, those luxuries could not distract him from the truth of the situation. He refused to stand by and allow his people's oppression to go unchecked. Overcome by a sense of injustice, Moses took action:

> Glancing this way and that and seeing no one, he killed the Egyptian and hid him in the sand.
>
> —Ex. 2:12

Moses was a man of conviction, discontent with the status quo, and indignant about the exploitation of his fellow Hebrews. He clenched his fists and literally took matters into his own hands, killing the Egyptian oppressor. Moses was so full of passion and courage as a young man that we might be inclined to see here an example of someone already playing for an Audience of One. We would be mistaken, though, and not just because he committed murder. There was an even more deeply seated problem with his passion and motivation: *it was completely self-generated.*

Not once in all of Exodus 2 did Moses ever call upon or even mention God in his effort to respond to his fellow Hebrews' oppression. He operated in his own strength without any divine direction or accountability. God was not Moses' Audience. God was not even on Moses' radar screen!

Moses was all about white-knuckling his way to results. I get that. As a recovering control freak, I can relate. If trying really hard to do things in my own strength were an Olympic event, I would have several gold medals.

As a child, I felt like it was my job to keep my parents from splitting up. I became so focused on doing everything I could (with clenched-fisted determination) to keep our family together that I lost sight of the fact that it wasn't my job to hold it all together. God loved my family more than I did—even in my very best moments.

As a dad, there are moments when I get so focused on trying to ensure my children's spiritual, emotional, and physical well being that I lose sight of the fact that God loves them more than I do. In fact, God is more concerned about my children's well being than I am—even in my very best moments.

As a pastor, there are times when I walk beside deep pain and see the hurt people are going through. I have a tendency to get so focused on doing everything I can to help them that sometimes I forget that God loves these people more than I do. In fact, God is more concerned about taking care of them than I am—even in my very best moments.

Hi, my name is Josh, and I'm a recovering control freak.

If I were in a twelve-step program, it would be for my addiction to control. Not that I try to control things for an evil end — usually when I get into clenched-fists mode, it's over things God cares about. The problem is when I try to manage those things in my own strength.

Playing for an Audience of One is not a license for unbridled zeal, where you do whatever you see fit as long as you do it passionately. Even your passion for doing things that are close to God's heart must be born out of a sense of what God is calling you to do. It's not enough that it's something you want to see happen–no matter how worthy the cause.

You and I probably haven't killed anyone, but how often are clenched fists the way we try to get things done? How often do we strive to accomplish something in our own strength? After all, sometimes clenching our fists "works." But not for long …

The day after Moses took matters into his own hands and killed the Egyptian, what he did was discovered. He became a marked man, and had to flee from Pharaoh into the desert, where he remained for the next four decades.

Does God Really Care?

That's when God showed up. God loves to show up and recruit people at unexpected times and in unexpected places. Showing up at a burning bush in the middle of the desert to an eighty-year-old fugitive-shepherd certainly qualified as an unexpected surprise. Perhaps even more surprising was what God first said to Moses — before He even asked him to do anything:

> I have indeed seen the misery of my people in Egypt. I have heard them crying out because of their slave drivers, and I am concerned about their suffering.
>
> —Ex. 3:7

This is significant. Remember, Moses had seen the Hebrew people's pain and suffering when he was back in Egypt. He had witnessed the beatings up close and personally. Whatever Moses thought about God during his final days in Egypt, he certainly must have concluded: *God doesn't care about the Hebrew people's pain and suffering. It's been almost four hundred years. He would have done something about it by now if He really cared.*

We've all been there, wondering to ourselves whether or not we care more than God does about the pain, suffering, and injustice we see in our world. We turn on the news and see the AIDS epidemic orphaning millions in Africa. We hear about the tens of thousands of little girls helplessly caught in the web of the prostitution trade in Southeast Asia. Closer to home, we have plenty of anecdotal evidence to support the theory that the bad guys get away with murder, while the good guys lose their jobs and get cancer. No wonder the psalmist confessed:

I saw the prosperity of the wicked. They have no struggles; their bodies are healthy and strong. They are free from the burdens common to man....Surely in vain I have kept my heart pure.

—Ps. 73:3-5, 13

We look at how the world operates and we understandably start to doubt whether God really cares.

Four hundred years of slavery certainly inclined Moses to wonder about God's concern for Israel. So when God showed up, He immediately corrected what Moses must have been thinking during his forty years in the desert. One of the first things God said to him was, "I do care, and I will do something." From there, God painted a picture of a preferred future for Israel:

I have come down to rescue them from the hand of the Egyptians and to bring them up out of that land into a good and spacious land, a land flowing with milk and honey.

—Ex. 3:8

God wanted Moses to know that His love for the Hebrews was not just a philosophical idea. It was real, and it was moving Him to do something about their situation: "I have come down to rescue them."

But before Moses could catch his breath, God said something else that seemed to contradict His promise of rescuing the Hebrews. God told Moses that *he* (Moses) was going to deliver the Hebrew people from Egypt:

So now, go. I am sending you to Pharaoh to bring My people the Israelites out of Egypt.

—Ex. 3:10

Now wait just a second. Didn't God say *He* was going to rescue the Hebrews? Then why did He call *Moses* to rescue them? Was God going to bring His people up out of Egypt or was Moses going to do it? The answer was yes! God was going to rescue His people out of Egypt, and He was going to use Moses to get it done. God was revealing to Moses that He not only cares, but He also shares. He wanted to share with Moses the privilege of rescuing a million Hebrews out of slavery.

Why would God seek to recruit Moses into this rescue mission? I mean God *is* all-powerful. He's more than able to pull off this emancipation of the slaves without Moses' help. Why would God even bother using an eighty-year-old fugitive?

It's true that God did not need Moses in any utilitarian sense. He doesn't need any of us to fulfill His mission in this world. And yet, the fact of the matter is that God takes great pleasure in inviting us to join Him in what He wants to get done. He wants us to share His heart and purpose for the world. That is precisely what was going on with Moses: the God of the universe was bidding Moses to leave his post as a desert shepherd, and join Him in the greatest rescue mission the world had ever known.

Handcuffed by Self-doubt

Moses didn't exactly jump at this once-in-a-lifetime invitation, though. His response says it all:

> Who am I, that I should I go to Pharaoh and bring the Israelites out
> of Egypt?
>
> —Ex. 3:11

You can hear the insecurity in his voice. What happened to the passion and conviction he had back in Exodus 2? Where is Moses' determination to stand up for the underdog, and speak out against the oppression of his people? This could have been his opportunity to redeem his earlier mistake in Egypt, and really do something meaningful in the world. Instead, he responded to God's invitation with the sheepish "Who am I?"

When Moses was back in Egypt, he was fists-clenched, white-knuckled, and boiling over with courage and conviction. Forty years later, he was handcuffed to self- doubt, and content to live out the rest of his days in the middle of the desert. His passion and zeal were gone. It's understandable. Moses had had a long time to dwell on his failed attempt back in Egypt.

That's how self-doubt does its real damage. Dwelling on past failure paralyzes us from trying again. Moses' deep insecurity was robbing him of the immense joy that comes from being used by God:

> We judge ourselves unworthy servants, and that judgment becomes a self-fulfilling prophecy. We deem ourselves too inconsiderable to be used even by a God capable of miracles with no more than mud and spit. And thus our false humility shackles an otherwise omnipotent God.[31]

It's Not About You, Moses!

God would not be so easily shackled, though. He responded to Moses' sheepish question of "Who am I?" the way He responds to all of us who wrestle with self-doubt and feelings of inadequacy:

> And God said, "*I* will be with you."
>
> —Ex. 3:12, emphasis mine

It's worth noting that God didn't try to convince Moses that he had latent leadership gifts. He didn't give Moses an inspiring pep talk about how he had the potential to become a world-class communicator. He didn't give Moses a lecture about the importance of maintaining a healthy self-esteem. God didn't play on that playing field at all. He simply responded to Moses' question of "Who am I?" by telling him, in essence, "It's not about you, Moses. It's about Me!"

I will be with you.

This was God's way of saying, "You're asking the wrong question, Moses. Lesson number one in your leadership training is this: What I call you to do is not primarily about you. It's about Me, so get over yourself!"

It's Not About You, Josh!

God has a way of reinforcing the lessons He wants us to learn. Whereas Moses needed to learn to get over himself through the arena of overcoming feelings of inadequacy, in my case, this lesson took the form of enduring a series of embarrassing moments—particularly during my first year as a pastor.

I remember the day I learned that our church's lapel microphones still worked even when we were outside the four walls of our sanctuary. It was a Sunday evening, moments before the service was to begin. The church was filled, and I had just made a brief pit stop at the restroom before I entered the sanctuary. (You probably know where this is going.)

As I stepped through the sanctuary doors, ready to lead the people in worship, I was greeted by a great big smile from our sound technician Brian, who was standing behind the sound booth and staring right at me. Puzzled by the smile on his face, I looked over at him with confusion written all over mine. He just kept grinning at me. Then I realized the reason for his wry smile. As I looked down at my microphone's on/off switch, it seemed to be flashing (in neon red): "ON! ON! ON!"

I'm sure my facial expression immediately changed from puzzled to mortified. I was a brand-new pastor and people were still making up their minds about me. My only hope was that perhaps Brian had caught my social faux pas and pushed the sound system's mute button while I was engaged in my restroom visit. The fact that he kept smiling at me, though, did not incline me to believe his grace had befallen me.

As I slowly approached the soundboard, Brian broke the silence, "So how was your trip to the bathroom?"

I didn't answer. I didn't even need to ask whether he had muted my microphone. My eyes clearly were pleading for the answer to that question.

Finally, after what seemed an eternity, Brian let me off the hook. "Don't worry about it," he said. "I muted your microphone."

I felt like launching into the Hallelujah Chorus right then and there! (Okay, so I didn't have to "get over myself" in front of the entire congregation, but I did have to do so for the sound tech! It's no wonder Brian and I became close friends. Embarrassing moments have a way of moving you from pseudo-community to genuine community.)

That was many years ago. If something like that happened today, and the sound tech forgot to push the mute button, I doubt I would react with so much panic. Hopefully, I've learned a little bit about getting over myself. I've certainly experienced enough embarrassing moments over the years to realize God can still do His thing through me even when I seem to get in the way. In fact, I've learned it's not really about me. But on that Sunday evening so many years ago, it certainly felt like it was. God's calling on my life (in that local church) seemed to hang in the balance of whether or not the sound tech pressed the mute button. Talk about narcissism!

Moses wasn't quite over himself yet, either. He still had another question he wanted to ask God:

> Suppose I go to the Israelites and say, "The God of your fathers has sent me to you," and they ask me, "What is His name?" Then what shall I tell them?
>
> —Ex. 3:13

Before Moses would go off and risk his neck in Egypt, he wanted to know a little more about this God who was calling him to lead the rescue mission. And again, God graciously answered his question, providing Moses with more knowledge of Him, and further insights into the plan of how He was going to bring the Hebrews out of Egypt. When God finished telling him the amazing plan for how He was going to set a million captives free and bring them into the Promised Land, Moses responded…with still more self-doubt:

> What if they do not believe me or listen to me?
>
> —Ex. 4:1

Despite God's invitation to be part of the most incredible rescue mission the world had ever known—he was still shackled to self-doubt. Moses couldn't seem to get over himself.

Getting Over Myself

I would be a hypocrite if I tried to vilify Moses. I have to confess how much I can relate to his story. I, too, remember struggling with whether or not I would ever be able to speak in front of a group of people—even years after I knew God had called me into the ministry.

Even though I could recall the euphoric feelings that went with His call on my life, and the sense of privilege I felt at being able to spend my life for such a meaningful purpose, I still felt handcuffed to my fears. Sure, I was excited to tell the world about Jesus, so long as I didn't have to say anything in front of a group of people!

My self-doubt reached its zenith when I dropped out of my public speaking class in college—three years after I had become certain of my calling. I rationalized to myself and to others that I was just "changing" classes in order to acquire a more convenient schedule. Deep down, though, I knew the real reason I was dropping the class: I was afraid my speaking ability wouldn't measure up to God's call on my life. More specifically, I was fearful people would hear me speak and say, "Are you sure God called you into the ministry?"

The problem didn't lie with my convictions. Like many Christians, I had a deep belief in the importance of God's rescue mission of the world. It's just that I couldn't seem to get over myself when it came to standing up in front of people and telling them about it.

How God Breaks the Shackles of Self-doubt

God was relentless in moving Moses toward obedience. He could have gotten someone else for the job, but He wanted Moses for this assignment. And God was prepared to pull out all the stops to break Moses' shackles of self-doubt. In fact, God's interaction with him in the next scene actually brought about the beginning of the end of those handcuffs. Moses still would struggle with self-doubt regarding his ability to lead the charge, but by the end of this conversation with God, he would sign on to be part of the greatest rescue mission the world had ever known. How God got him there is instructive for the rest of us who are still bound by the shackles of self-doubt.

1. *Recognize what you have*

Up to this point in the story, Moses had been the one asking all of the questions. Then God had one of his own, a question that would change Moses' life forever:

"What is that in your hand?" God asked.

—Ex 4:2a

It seemed a simple enough question, but it was actually intended to draw Moses into an experience of the way God works.

"A staff," Moses replied.

—Ex. 4:2b

Don't overlook this inventory assessment question. The first step in Moses' getting over himself was helping him *recognize* he had something God could use. It could have been anything: an ordinary nail, a chocolate candy bar, a paperclip, or a stick of gum. In Moses' case, it was his staff - just a seemingly insignificant staff. But it was something, and that little something was all God needed to do His thing.

2. *Surrender it to God*

The next step God wanted Moses to take with his staff was even more important:

The Lord said, "Throw it on the ground." Moses threw it on the ground and it became a snake, and he ran from it.

—Ex. 4:3

The second step in breaking the power of self-doubt was getting Moses to *surrender* what he was holding onto. It was not enough for Moses to recognize what he had in his hand. He also needed to throw it at God's feet in an act of surrender.

A word of caution to those Christians who are infatuated with figuring out their spiritual gifts: you can take every spiritual gift inventory ever designed, but if you are not fully yielded to God, those tests are just exercises in religious narcissism. Many of us want God to lead and use us, but we fail to see the connection between God using us, and this all-important step of surrender.

This step of surrender finally happened for me when I signed on to do a summer internship in inner city Detroit, just a couple of months after dropping out of my college speech class. Part of the reason I looked into doing the internship was I finally admitted to myself that I needed to do something drastic to get over myself. I knew in this particular ministry setting I would be forced to deal with my feelings of insecurity. The senior pastor of this church had a reputation for pushing interns out of their comfort zones. What an understatement!

For instance, I remember the time the church's worship leader was a no-show. Less than an hour before the service was to begin, the pastor informed me I would be leading worship that night. I just about wet my pants when he gave me the assignment. I had only started playing the guitar about three months earlier. I had never led worship before. That night I did so on about forty-five minutes' notice. You see, I couldn't bail. I was living in the pastor's basement that summer—so there was nowhere for me to run! I'm not going to lie. It wasn't a tightly led worship service with beautifully orchestrated segues. The worship service wasn't pretty at all. But I did it. And the experience was exactly what I needed, too. The handcuffs of self-doubt loosened a bit that night.

That summer I was also part of the ministry team that did neighborhood evangelism events for kids. Normally, the "real" pastors would give the gospel presentation at these gatherings. But one afternoon, about fifteen minutes before the program was to begin, the children's pastor commissioned me, the intern, to give the gospel message. Again, there was no preparation time. There was no wiggle room, either—no way to conveniently "change classes" to mask my fear of speaking in front of people. I just had to do it. So I did. And I know for a fact that at least one kid got saved that day: *me!*

The handcuffs of self-doubt continued to loosen.

God is both patient and persistent in dealing with our tendency to kick and scream against His call on our lives. He does not let us get away with viewing our self-doubt as a legitimate reason for resistance. A full surrender means relinquishing even our inadequacy and insecurity if we're using them as an excuse for delaying obedience. If that's your tendency, then perhaps what you need is to voluntarily put yourself in a position where you know you'll be forced to get over yourself.

That summer changed my life because it forced me to begin taking steps that I never would have taken otherwise. And it began with surrender. I yielded myself to God (and to the senior pastor of that inner city church in Detroit). As a result, I began to experience the Spirit's help to do those things I knew He wanted me to do. It also deepened my prayer life. After all, nothing moves us to prayer like desperation! And nothing catalyzes desperation like putting up the white flag and surrendering ourselves to do whatever God asks us to do.

In a sense, putting up the white flag means a death to self, what Oswald Chambers, the author of *My Utmost for His Highest*, calls attending one's own "white funeral."[32] Chambers calls us to venture to the edge of our own open grave by asking this haunting question:

> Is there a place in your life marked as the last day, a place to which the memory goes back with a chastened and extraordinarily grateful remembrance, "Yes, it was then, at the white funeral, that I made an agreement with God."[33]

If you truly are seeking to play for an Audience of One, this step of surrender is not an option. Just as God continued to prod Moses to obedience, He will woo you to a full and complete surrender. God is patiently insistent on this point, but in the end He will not force your hand. It's your choice. He refuses to take away your free will. As C.S. Lewis says, "There are only two kinds of people in the end: those who say to God, 'Thy will be done,' and those to whom God says, 'Thy will be done.'"[34]

God did not coerce Moses to take this step of surrender. He invited him to throw down his staff. But in the end, it was Moses who actually had to do it.

3. *Take up the staff again (and watch God work through it!)*

Surrender isn't the finish line of the spiritual journey, though. There was still something else God wanted Moses to do. While that seemingly insignificant staff was lying on the ground, God did something to it that changed it forever—which is why He then asked Moses to do one more thing. The third step in breaking the power of the handcuffs came when God called Moses to *take up* the staff again:

Then the Lord said to him, "Reach out your hand and take it by the tail." So Moses reached out and took hold of the snake and it turned back into a staff in his hand. "This," said the Lord, "is so that they may believe."

—Ex. 4:4-5

Of all the things God could have used, why did He use this staff? Think about what "this staff" represented for Moses. "This staff" was no mere walking stick. Remember how the story began: "Now Moses was tending the flock" (Ex. 3:1). Moses was a shepherd. "This staff" was Moses' shepherd's staff. It represented his job. It symbolized his vocation. It was what he did. But it represented even more than that. Moses' very identity was wrapped up in this shepherd's staff. It symbolized who he thought he was and who he thought he never could be.

When Moses asked God the question, "Who am I?" he wasn't looking for an answer. It was a rhetorical question. Moses already "knew" the answer to his own question. Every time he looked down at what he was holding in his hand, Moses' shepherd's staff reminded him exactly who he was: *Lord, I'm a nobody. Forty years ago, I proved I'm a failure. I'm just a shepherd, and I have this shepherd's staff in my hand to prove it. Go find someone else with a more impressive résumé.*

That's all Moses thought he was, and that's exactly why God called him to throw down his staff and pick it up again. In a sense, this was God's way of getting Moses to throw down himself, so he would get back up a new and changed man. In the act of surrendering his staff, Moses was symbolically surrendering his vocation and identity to God. And once that shepherd's staff got thrown down before God, it was never the same.

What Can God Do with a Surrendered Staff?

Once that shepherd's staff hit the ground, God's touch transformed it forever. When Moses took it up again, it was no longer fit simply to tend sheep. This shepherd's staff became God's chosen instrument for rescuing a million human beings out of slavery, and bringing them into relationship with Him. As Tozer writes, "Whatever is given to Christ is immediately touched with immortality."[35] That's why at the end of this conversation God tells Moses:

Make sure that you take this staff in your hand so that you can perform miraculous signs with it!

—Ex. 4:17

Reading through the rest of Exodus, we discover that this shepherd's staff:

- Became a snake, and swallowed all of the staffs of Pharaoh's sorcerers (7:10)
- Turned the Nile River into blood (7:19)
- Initiated the plague of frogs (8:5)
- Set off the plague of gnats (8:16)
- Launched the plague of hail (9:23)
- Inaugurated the plague of locusts (10:13)
- Parted the Red Sea (14:15)
- Brought forth enough water from a rock for a million thirsty people (17:5)
- Secured the Israelites' military victory over the Amalekites (17:9)

How did a seemingly insignificant shepherd's staff do all of this? Because Moses threw it down before the One who can use anything and anyone to accomplish His purposes. In this simple act of obedient surrender, Moses' staff became consecrated to God. The staff became supernaturally anointed to do whatever God wanted it to do. *Once God gets His hands on something, it can be anything—it's just a matter of time before He accomplishes His mission with it.*

A New Name

From this point on in the story, Moses' shepherd's staff had a new name:

Moses…started back to Egypt. And he took the *staff of God* in his hand.

—Ex. 4:20, emphasis mine

For the rest of the story, the shepherd's staff would be referred to as "the staff of God!" It had been transformed, given new meaning and purpose, and fitted for God's rescue mission. God can do that with anything surrendered to Him. *Whatever is given to Christ is immediately touched with immortality.*

What's in your hand? Remember, the size and apparent significance of your "staff" makes no difference to God. He can use you regardless of your gifts, personality type, or lack of self-confidence. God's invitation to Moses is the same invitation He extends to you: surrender all of yourself to all of Him, willingly throwing down whatever you possess at His feet, and then see what He will do with it. It's only then that God can do through you all He wants to do.

As the ancient Chinese saying goes, "The journey of a thousand miles begins with the first step." Make no mistake. The first step in the journey toward playing for an Audience of One is surrender. No wonder Chambers' *My Utmost for His Highest* begins the way it does. Here's an excerpt from his January 1 entry:

> My determination is to be my utmost for His highest. To get there is
> a question of will, not of debate, nor of reasoning, but a surrender of
> will, an absolute and irrevocable surrender on that point.[36]

Whether you're eight years old or eighty, you don't have to spend another day wandering aimlessly in the desert, clutching onto your staff. God is inviting you to throw it down and join Him in the most important thing that is happening on planet Earth: the rescue mission of the human race, reconciling the world to God through the good news of Jesus. And you can play a meaningful role in this rescue mission, even if your staff is simply used to "turn little omelets in the pan for the love of God." He can use that, too, if it's been given over to Him.

The Impact of 'Our Surrendering' on the World

John Wesley, whom God used to spearhead the English revival in the eighteenth century, said:

> Give me one hundred preachers who fear nothing but sin and desire
> nothing but God, and I care not a straw whether they be clergy or

laymen, such alone will shake the gates of hell, and set up the Kingdom of heaven on earth.[37]

This same principle is true on the individual level. I've heard it said that one person who is 100 percent consecrated to God is of greater use for the kingdom than a hundred people who are 90 percent consecrated to God. It's true.

Don't underestimate what the Spirit can do through someone who is fully consecrated to God. Take D. L. Moody, for instance. He was one of the greatest evangelists in the church's history. Hundreds of thousands of believers today trace their spiritual roots to his ministry. However, it was an early episode in his life, before he became famous, that tells the story of why God could use him so powerfully:

> When Moody was young, an Irish friend named Henry Varley told him, "Moody, the world has yet to see what God will do with a man fully consecrated to Him." Moody was startled by the statement. He kept thinking about it for days. He reasoned: "A man! Varley meant *any* man. Varley didn't say he had to be educated, or brilliant, or anything else. Just a man. Well, by the Holy Spirit in me, I will be that man!"[38]

Moody recognized what he brought to God: he was just a simple human being. But nevertheless he surrendered himself wholly and completely to God. Moody threw himself on the ground before God. And when he picked himself back up off the ground the world indeed saw what God could do with someone fully consecrated to Him.

God might call you into overseas missions work. He might call you into pastoral ministry. He might call you into a marketplace vocation where you can influence the world for Christ in ways that traditional forms of ministry cannot. He might call you to stay right where you are and invest the rest of your life serving in your local church and being salt and light in your sphere of influence. Regardless of the specifics of His calling, though, God cannot and will not do fully what He wants to do in and through you until you first throw down whatever is in your hand. But when that happens, look out: *The world has yet to see what God will do through someone fully consecrated to Him!*

Prayer of Surrender

Take my life and let it be consecrated, Lord, to Thee.

—Frances Ridley Havergal

Going Deeper

1. Do a personal inventory on the question, "What's in your hand?" Take some time to recognize your gifts, talents, job, resources, fears, and insecurities. How would you define your "staff"?
2. Surrender your "staff" (yourself) to God. Plan your own "white funeral," where you prepare something in writing to memorialize the day.
3. Take up your staff (yourself), trusting that God has given you a new name. No longer are you to view yourself as insignificant. You are now to see yourself as "man of God" or "woman of God." Then watch God do His thing in and through you!

Chapter 5

SOMETIMES FAITHFULNESS LEADS TO "FAILURE"

"And now I have no one, no one but God."[39]

—Dixon Hoste

MICHAEL JORDAN, A six-time NBA champion, five-time league Most Valuable Player, and considered by many to be the most dominant basketball player ever to play the game, said, "I've missed more than nine thousand shots in my career. I've lost almost three hundred games. Twenty-six times, I've been trusted to take the game winning shot and missed. I've failed over and over again in my life. And that is why I succeed."[40]

Brett Favre was a Super Bowl champion, an NFL three-time Most Valuable Player, a nine-time Pro-Bowler, and the record holder for the most career touchdowns thrown (442). Unfortunately, the Iron Man of Football's stat sheet is not without its blemishes. Brett also threw 288 interceptions over the course of his career, good for first place all-time in that dubious category.

Hank Aaron was a twenty-one-time All Star, a National League MVP, and (for 33 years) the owner of the most recognizable feat in sports: the all-time homerun record. Hank blasted 755 homeruns during his illustrious career—without the assistance of steroids! But...he also struck out 1,383 times, nearly twice for every homerun he hit.

Are you seeing a pattern?

There is a saying among baseball players that even those who fail 70 percent of the time still make the Hall of Fame. In other words, a player who hits safely just 30 percent of the time (.300) over the course of his career has a very good chance of achieving the most prestigious honor in baseball: an induction into the Hall of Fame at Cooperstown. But that accomplishment only happens for those who are willing to fail a majority of the time—year in and year out.

Failure comes with the territory, even for Hall of Famers.

If an athlete's goal is never to fail, there is only one sure-fire way to achieve that objective: never step into the batter's box, never take a snap under center, and never attempt a shot. Of course, ballplayers who take that approach will never hit any homeruns, never throw any touchdowns and never make any game-winning baskets. The truly great athletes know that missed shots, interceptions, and strikeouts come with the territory. Failure is just a given part of the journey toward winning championships and achieving long-range success. That is why Michael Jordan could say so confidently, "I've failed over and over again in my life. And that is why I succeed."

The Prosperity Gospel in the Form of Success

Unfortunately, many of us in the church don't know how to stomach failure. We have bought into a version of the gospel that has no appreciation for failure's role in the spiritual journey. We want every swing of the bat to be a homerun. We think that, with Jesus, success should mark every aspect of our lives. Not that we're looking to be on the cover of *Forbes* or interviewed on the next episode of "Lifestyles of the Rich and Famous." We're not that selfish. We just want the decisions we make to go well, the dreams we dream to come true, the prayers we pray to be answered, and all our relationships to be satisfying and pain-free. Is that so much to ask?

There's nothing inherently wrong with desiring success. It's when we think success is our spiritual birthright that we get into trouble.

What happens when life doesn't play out the way we expected? If you're like me, you begin to wonder where things went wrong. You become discouraged and confused. You second-guess yourself, and then you second-guess God. You and I do this, in large part, because we have bought into the tantalizing lie that if we have Jesus on our side, *and we do what He says*, then our lives will be marked by success. This lie is just another form of the prosperity gospel, and its origin is the pit of hell.

When some form of "failure" eventually comes your way, and it will, you probably will come to one of these conclusions:

- "I must have done something wrong. Perhaps I didn't hear God correctly. Maybe I didn't pray enough, or maybe I didn't stay in step with the Spirit. Somewhere along the way, *I* blew it."
- "God must not have kept up His end of the bargain. I did what I was supposed to do, and yet things still didn't work out. The only other explanation for this 'failure,' then, is God let me down. *God* blew it."

Notice I am putting quotation marks around the word *failure*. The effects of your obedience to God may cause you to think of yourself as a failure from a human perspective, but that is never His view on the matter. There will be occasions when your faithfulness to do what God asks you to do may result in what looks like failure. But that wouldn't be the first time that's happened among God's people.

Faithfulness Leads to "Failure" in the Bible

A quick perusal of the Scriptures reveals that this theme of faithfulness leading to apparent failure runs throughout the whole biblical story:

- Jeremiah's obedience to God led him into imprisonment by his own people. He faithfully preached God's Word, but in terms of gaining a successful hearing, Jeremiah failed. Israel refused to respond to his messages. They outright rejected him again and again. No wonder Jeremiah was called "the weeping prophet."
- Job's obedience to God led him to suffer tremendous physical, emotional, and spiritual pain. According to his friends (and the conventional wisdom of the day), Job's life of hardships was clear evidence he had blown it somewhere along the way.
- Hosea's obedience to God led to marital rejection. His fidelity was rewarded with loneliness, adultery, and betrayal. I doubt if

Hosea ever got invited to speak at many Focus on the Family seminars!

- John the Baptist's obedience to God led him to prison and death.
- The early church's obedience to God often led them into persecution and martyrdom.

This isn't my favorite theme in the Bible, but I can't deny that it's there. The fact that we often overlook or ignore this motif of faithfulness leading to "failure" betrays our love affair with success. We prefer stories from the Bible like David defeating Goliath, or Elijah overpowering the 450 false prophets of Baal. But the truth is, sometimes faithfulness to God leads to apparent failure. This is not without reason. Nothing tests a person's mettle like failure. Failure not only serves to teach humility and perseverance, it is one of the primary means by which God finds out how badly we want to play for an Audience of One. After all, if you experienced success every time you were obedient to God, you might be inclined to obey Him simply as a means to personal achievement.

T. S. Eliot said the greatest sin is to do the right thing for the wrong reason.[41] That might be overstating the severity of the issue, but it certainly puts the spotlight on a dimension of our spiritual lives that God takes very seriously: our motives. Nothing draws out the poison of impure motives like a good dose of failure. Failure is one of God's commonly prescribed antidotes for purging from us the tendency to do the right thing for the wrong reason. Few people have ever been injected with as much of the "failure antidote" as Moses was. He's become an inspiration to me for how to respond to apparent failure when I've been faithful to do what God has asked me to do.

"We Don't Want Your Help!"

As we saw in the previous chapter, Moses eventually learned the lesson of surrender. In the act of throwing his shepherd's staff to the ground, it became "the staff of God." It was anointed to perform miraculous signs. From there, Moses picked up his staff, went to Egypt, and relayed to Pharaoh the message from God: "Let my people go" (Ex. 5:1).

Given all of Moses' feelings of insecurity and self-doubt, it's important not to gloss over this detail. This step of obedience was huge. For Moses to take this message to the commander in chief of the world's greatest superpower took guts. You might think God would have been gracious in rewarding Moses' first act of obedience with some positive reinforcement. You know, to shore up Moses' apprehension about whether or not he could really do what God was calling him to do. But that's not what happened. Notice the response Moses got from Pharaoh after doing what he was supposed to do: "The King of Egypt said, 'Moses and Aaron, why are you taking the people away, from their labor? Get back to your work'" (Ex. 5:4)!

Pharaoh's biting response wouldn't have come as a big surprise to Moses. God had forewarned him that Pharaoh would harden his heart against the message. More discouraging was how Moses' own people responded. That's what really threw him into a temporary tailspin:

> That same day Pharaoh gave this order to the slave drivers and foremen in charge of the people: "You are no longer to supply the people with straw for making bricks; let them go and gather their own straw. But require them to make the same number of bricks as before; don't reduce the quota."
>
> …The Israelite foremen realized they were in trouble.
>
> —Ex. 5:6-8, 19

Pretend you are an Israelite foreman, and you don't know the rest of the Exodus story. How would you rate the effectiveness of Moses' first act of leadership? On a scale of one to ten, what kind of score would you give him? Be honest. Your people are still in bondage. The slavery conditions are even worse today than they were yesterday. In fact, the only difference between yesterday's manageable brick quotas and today's impossible workload is Moses' negotiation talk with Pharaoh.

I know what kind of score I would have given Moses.

Suffice it to say that the Israelite foremen were not impressed with the leadership of their new labor union president. Here's what they wrote in the "comments" section of Moses' evaluation form:

> May the Lord look upon you and judge you! You have made us a stench to Pharaoh and his officials and have put a sword in their hand to kill us.
>
> —Ex. 5:20-21

The foremen wanted to run Moses out of Egypt before he could make their lives any worse. Sound reminiscent of the first time Moses tried to help his people?

Think about the memories that must have been surfacing in Moses' mind as he listened to the complaints of his fellow Israelites. No doubt he could still vividly recall those words uttered by another Hebrew, the one he had tried to help when he was in Egypt some forty years earlier: "Who made you ruler and judge over us" (Ex. 2:14)?

Moses was back in Egypt, trying to help his fellow Hebrews again, and here he was getting the very same response he had gotten forty years earlier: *Who do you think you are? What makes you think you have anything to offer? We don't want your help!* This is not the kind of pep talk that gives confidence to someone struggling with insecurity and self-doubt. It's one thing when the enemy is angry with you. That's to be expected. But it's another thing when your own people don't want anything to do with you. Moses was experiencing rejection by both sides: from Pharaoh and from his own people.

God Deals with the Ghosts of our Past

Here was the lesson: God wanted Moses to learn to trust Him amidst the resentment and rejection of his fellow Hebrews. God knew Moses' past. He knew failure and rejection were sensitive issues for Moses. But God was relentless in doing what needed to be done to move Moses to a place of total dependence upon Him—as opposed to letting him keep leaning on the opinions of the Hebrew people for support and direction. How else would Moses be able to lead the people of Israel through the wilderness during those years of constant grumbling and complaining? God wanted a leader who would stay the course even when his public approval rating took a hit. So God brought Moses face-to-face with the ghosts of his past in order to see how he would respond to rejection and apparent failure.

Back at the burning bush, God had given Moses all sorts of inside information about how the Exodus story was going to unfold:

- Pharaoh would harden his heart.
- It would take plagues to get Pharaoh to let the people go.
- The Hebrews would plunder the Egyptians before they left Egypt.
- God would bring them into the Promised Land, a land flowing with milk and honey.

But God never told Moses the part of the story where his own people reject him and his leadership.

Perhaps God knew Moses never would have gone to Egypt if he had known about this little detail of the story. God put Moses into the very situation where he would have to face his fear of failure, and the pain of being rejected again by his own people. Not only did Pharaoh's mandate make the work harder for the Hebrew slaves, but the hostile words from the Israelite foremen served as a double-blow to Moses' already shaky trust in his calling.

But God was using this apparent failure to do a deep work in Moses.

Faithfulness to God May Cost Others

It's understandable that the Hebrews would be so angry with Moses. After all, his meeting with Pharaoh did make their slavery conditions worse. From their perspective, they could do without this kind of help. But God wasn't interested solely in setting the Hebrews free from the tyranny of their master: the Egyptians. He was just as determined to set Moses free from the tyranny of his master: the opinions of his own people. In order for God to do this deeper work in Moses, though, the Hebrew people would be inflicted with even more pain, and Moses would have to deal with the fact that it was his obedience to God that was catalyzing it.

One of the lessons Moses had to learn was that our faithfulness to God sometimes causes pain in the lives of those around us. As Oswald Chambers writes:

If we obey God, it is going to cost other people more than it costs us, and that is where the sting comes in. If we are in love with our Lord, obedience does not cost us anything—it is a delight. But to those who do not love Him, our obedience does cost a great deal. If we obey God it will mean that other people's plans are upset, and they will ridicule us with it, "You call this Christianity?" We could prevent the suffering, but not if we are obedient to God. We must let the cost be paid.[42]

For some of us, the idea of absorbing pain is much easier to deal with than causing it. Most of us would prefer to bear the cross all by ourselves than burden someone else with it. For the most part, this is the way it should work. But there will be points in your journey when God will ask you to do things that will impact others in ways they will not like. Your obedience to God may grieve, frustrate, or disappoint them. The question is whether you will stay true to His calling despite the pain your obedience is inflicting on them, or whether you will let your proud refusal to cause someone else pain dictate the path you take. As Chambers continues:

Because we are so involved in the universal purposes of God, others are immediately affected by our obedience to Him....We can disobey God if we choose, and it will bring immediate relief to the situation, but we shall be a grief to our Lord. Whereas if we obey God, He will look after those who have been pressed into the consequences of our obedience. We have simply to obey and to leave all consequences with Him.[43]

Make no mistake about it. There will be times in the journey when your obedience to God will cost other people:

- A confrontation you sense God leading you to initiate may hurt someone's feelings.
- A decision God has been speaking to you about regarding the purity of the entertainment in your home may trigger frustration and confusion in your children.
- Sharing the gospel with a neighbor or a co-worker may offend them.

- A conviction about pursuing a simpler lifestyle may cause resentment among those in your family who previously enjoyed the amenities your money could buy.
- A geographic move that God is calling you to make may disappoint family members and friends.

For some of us, there is nothing that feels more like "failure" than knowing something we did caused another person pain. Can you play for an Audience of One even when God asks you to do that which might cause someone else pain? Can you trust that God will look after those who have been "pressed into the consequences of our obedience," or will you seek immediate relief, and in so doing "become a grief to our Lord"?

That was the test for Moses.

Dealing with Failure in God's Presence

Moses did not seek the immediate relief that would have come had he just thrown in the towel and gone back to his shepherd post in the desert. He was understandably confused by the turn of events. After finally surrendering to God and being obedient to Him, his life got *harder*, not easier. Not only that, but the situation for his fellow Hebrews got *worse*, not better. Instead of bailing, though, Moses stayed and prayed. His prayer is an awesome example of how we can respond to apparent failure:

> O Lord, why have you brought trouble upon this people? Is this why You sent me? Ever since I went to Pharaoh to speak in Your name, he has brought trouble upon this people, and You have not rescued Your people at all.
>
> —Ex. 5:22-23

What a great prayer: honest, unpretentious, straightforward. Moses laid his disappointment and frustration on the table before God. Granted, it's not exactly the prayer of a spiritual giant. Moses' complaint reflects a very limited view of what God was up to. His prayer is also motivated, at least in part, by his own sense of rejection by the Hebrew people. But this much can be said for Moses: *at least he took his frustration and his feelings of failure to the One who could provide perspective about what was going on.*

Regardless of all the mixed motives that inspired Moses' prayer of frustration, the fact of the matter is: Moses prayed. He took his sense of failure to God, and he struggled with it in His presence. And because Moses was willing to deal with his apparent failure this way, he opened himself up to the encouragement and perspective that God wants to give all of us who feel the pain of disappointment and failure. Notice what God said to Moses next:

> Then the Lord said to Moses, "Now you will see what I will do to Pharaoh: Because of My mighty hand he will let them go; because of My mighty hand he will drive them out of his country....Moreover, I have heard the groaning of the Israelites, whom the Egyptians are enslaving, and I have remembered my covenant."
>
> —Ex. 6:1, 5

God assured Moses that the plan had not changed: the Hebrews would be set free from their slavery. He had not forgotten His covenant with Israel. The message God was gaving Moses was this: *Moses, you have not blown it, and neither have I! Don't get short sighted about what's going on. Keep the long-range perspective. What feels like failure is not really failure. Stay the course, and you'll see.*

By the end of the conversation, Moses was reminded of the big picture and inspired to keep on track. The encouragement wouldn't have come, though, without Moses taking his frustration to God in prayer. Moses was reeling from a sense of rejection. He was angry and disappointed at the outcome of his first act of obedience, but he took those feelings of failure to God.

If you're like me, you might be tempted to respond to failure by:

- Putting your tail between your legs, and feeling so much shame that you never talk about it.
- Spinning the failure, and making it sound like everything happened "just as planned."

- Avoiding or resenting God—especially if you know you were obedient to Him.
- Resolving to play it safe, and never put yourself in a situation where you might fail again.

How do you deal with failure? Do you work through your disappointment in God's presence or do you "take care of it" in one of these ways? Is there any failure in your past that you have not taken to God? If so, stop reading and do business with God about it now—even if you're still angry or frustrated. He's big enough to listen to your complaint. Take your lead from the psalmist, who prayed:

> Hear me, O God, as I voice my complaint.
>
> —Ps. 64:1

The Allure of Spiritual Success

The reason so many of us fall apart upon meeting up with some form of failure is that we have a distorted view of God and how He works. Our perspective of what is really going on is particularly blurry when our failure results from a sincere attempt to do something we know God was asking us to do. Somehow this kind of failure is all the more devastating to us. We feel more shame, a stronger inclination to spin the story of what happened, a deeper sense of resentment, and a greater determination to never risk for God again. For some of us, experiencing failure in a spiritual context is the worst kind of failure. Why?

We view this kind of failure as a reflection on our relationship with God. In other words, we assume our failure means that somehow we must have fallen short of what God asked us to do. On the other hand, when things go well for us in an assignment from God (and we all have our own definition of what "going well" means), we deduce that His favor and approval must be resting upon us. But God's lines of success and failure are not so clear-cut. That's why Jesus warned His disciples against the allure of seeking after success—even success in a ministry context.

In Luke 10, the disciples came back from their short-term mission trip on cloud nine. They were excited because they had been casting out demons and seeing people respond to the their preaching. Jesus interrupted their celebration, though, to give them some much-needed perspective about what was really important: "Do not rejoice that the spirits submit to you, but rejoice that your names are written in heaven" (Luke 10:20). Jesus wanted to ensure that His disciples didn't make more of their ministry "success" than they ought. It's not evil to be excited about success. But if that's your primary means of being inspired to obey God, you will be tempted to bail on Him when things don't go the way you want them to go.

Obedience Is the Non-negotiable

A disclaimer is required at this point. The solution to the mixed motives that churn within you is not to stop doing anything until your motives are as pure as the driven snow. If you wait for that day, you will never do anything. You'll be forever paralyzed by the fear that there may be some ulterior motive lurking behind everything you do. You'll second-guess everything you do. Your desire to obey God with perfectly pure motives will handcuff you from doing what He asks.

The solution to the mixed motive problem is not to stop doing that for which you have mixed motives. Rather, it is to obey God, and then be consistent in calling out the impure motives when you sense them inspiring your actions. You don't need to go on a witch-hunt in search of your impure motives. If you are seeking to play for an Audience of One, God will shine His spotlight on them. You simply need to respond: by getting honest with yourself about them, surrendering them to God, and then sharing them with a trusted friend for prayer and accountability.

If you are consistently confessing and surrendering these impure motives, then your obedience to God will begin to be marked with greater freedom from mixed motives. It doesn't happen overnight. But it never will happen if you make pure motives the prerequisite for obeying. Obedience to God is the non-negotiable. Refusing to obey God until all of your mixed motives get purified will only delay or completely short-circuit your obedience. Obedience to God (with mixed motives) is still better than disobedience. Let's work on our mixed motives *while* we obey God.

Inspiration Leads to Perspiration

We're often tempted to think that once we learn something God will allow us to move on to the next lesson. But rarely, in my experience, is once enough to solidify what God wants me to learn. It usually takes a few times before I get it.

After God gave Moses a renewed vision of his mission and a reprieve from the rejection and hostility of the Hebrew people, He told Moses to go right back to the Hebrews with the same message:

> Therefore, say to the Israelites, "I am the LORD, and I will bring you out from under the yoke of the Egyptians. I will free you from being slaves."
>
> —Ex. 6:6

This was the moment of truth for Moses. Would he go back to those who had rejected his leadership? Would he risk further disappointment? Would he put himself in a position where he might fail again? It's one thing to be inspired by a vision from God while "up on the mountain" on a weekend retreat. It's another thing to come down that mountain and live out that vision in the valley of human opposition on Monday morning. That's what God was looking for from Moses, though. After all, inspiration is always meant to lead to perspiration.

> We have all experienced times of exaltation on the mountain, when we have seen things from God's perspective and have wanted to stay there. But God will never allow us to stay there. The true test of our spiritual life is in exhibiting the power to descend from the mountain....It is a wonderful thing to be on the mountain with God, but a person only gets there so that he may later go down and lift up the demon-possessed people in the valley. We are not made for the mountains, for sunrises, or for the other beautiful attractions in life—those are simply intended to be moments of inspiration. We are made for the valley and the ordinary things of life, and that is where we have to prove our stamina and strength.[44]

Moses did "come down the mountain." He went back to the Hebrew people, risked further failure and rejection, and relayed to them God's message. Unfortunately, their response was no different than before:

Moses reported this to the Israelites, but they did not listen to him because of their discouragement and cruel bondage.

—Ex. 6:9

Imagine what a kick in the gut it must have been for Moses to obey God again, only to be met with still more rejection from his own people. What must Moses have been thinking at this point? If he had doubts about his communication skills before, I'm sure his inability to compel the Israelites to listen to him now was like the nail in the coffin. And just when we might expect another inspirational speech from God, we get nothing of the kind. Instead of more encouragement and a reminder about keeping perspective, God simply follows up the Israelites' rejection by giving Moses his next speaking assignment:

Then the Lord said to Moses, "Go, tell Pharaoh king of Egypt to let the Israelites go out of his country."

—Ex. 6:10-11

This was final exam time for Moses. Think about what he must have been feeling when he heard God's next assignment. I know what I would have been thinking: *I don't even have the allegiance of my own people yet, and now You're sending me to Pharaoh again!*
Understandably, Moses slipped back into self-doubt:

But Moses said to the Lord, "If the Israelites will not listen to me, why would Pharaoh listen to me, since I speak with faltering lips?"

—Ex. 6:12

Translation: *How many times do I have to experience rejection and failure before the elephant in the room gets acknowledged? Nobody is listening to me! Okay, Lord, You predicted ahead of time that Pharaoh wouldn't listen, but my own people have rejected me twice! You didn't say anything about that. Remember back at the burning bush, when I told You nobody would listen to me? Well, I told you so!*

Keep Swinging the Bat

Moses still assumed that the people's response was the measuring stick that determined whether or not he should continue on in the journey. We shouldn't be too hard on Moses. It's difficult to play for an Audience of One when everyone in the auditorium of life is screaming for you to get off the stage! But God wanted to shape Moses into a leader who wasn't driven to despair when his public approval rating plummeted. History's greatest leaders have been refined in the fires of failure.

Abraham Lincoln first attempted a career in business in 1831 and failed miserably. A year later he ran for state legislature unsuccessfully. The same year he lost his job and applied to law school but was laughed out of consideration because of his miserable qualifications. Not long after that humiliating ordeal, he started another business using money he borrowed from a close friend. Lincoln claimed bankruptcy and spent the next seventeen years paying off debt.

In 1835 he fell deeply in love with Ann Rutledge, only to have his heart broken when she died soon after their engagement. The following year he had a complete nervous breakdown and spent the next six months in bed recovering.

In 1838 he sought to become speaker of the state legislature and was defeated.

In 1840, two years later, he sought to become the elector of the state, and was defeated. Three years later he ran for Congress and lost.

In 1846 he ran again for Congress and won. Only two years later he ran for reelection and was soundly defeated.

In 1849 he sought the job of land officer in his home state but was rejected.

In 1854 he ran for the Senate of the United States. Again, he lost.

In 1856 he sought the vice-presidential nomination at his party's national convention. He got less than one hundred votes, suffering yet another embarrassing defeat.

In 1858 he ran for the U.S. Senate and lost again.

Finally in 1860 Abraham Lincoln was elected to the presidency of the United States and soon after endured the most devastating war our country has ever experienced....We reflect on a presidency like his and our tendency is to think, *my, what a magnificent background he must have had.* Then we peer deeper into the dark cave of his past and realize it's riddled with failure.[45]

God wanted to make Moses into a leader who wouldn't hang up his cleats after a couple of early-inning strikeouts. After all, you can't hit homeruns if your only goal is to never, ever strikeout. Herman Melville wrote, "He who has never failed somewhere, that man cannot be great. Failure is the test of greatness."[46]

Sometimes the best preparation for long-term success is initial failure.

Things Are Not What They Seem

We would do well to remember that things are not always what they seem. We do not always see (on this side of heaven) what our obedience to God means for the kingdom. We should suspend judgment about the kingdom-value of our "failure" or the worth of our seemingly insignificant service. After all, there will be surprises when we get to heaven as to the real importance of what we did for the Lord: "Lord, when did we…feed you…clothe you…visit you" (Matt. 25:37-38)?

Besides that, not everyone who surrenders to God gets to be used like Billy Graham. Playing for an Audience of One does not mean you will always (or ever) be used in outwardly "successful" ways. In fact, some would argue that God gets more glory when you serve Him in behind-the-scenes ways.

A man once approached Mother Teresa and said, "Mother, I want to do something great for God, but I don't know what. Should I start a school, be a missionary in a foreign land, or build up a charitable agency?" This man had grand visions. He really wanted his life to make a difference. But Mother Teresa looked at him closely, and with kindness in her voice, responded, "What you need to do is make sure that no one

SOMETIMES FAITHFULNESS LEADS TO "FAILURE"   83

in your family goes unloved." Mother Teresa was always being asked about how one could have a great impact on this world for God. She would frequently respond with, "In this life we cannot do great things for God. We can only do small things for God with great love."[47] *Playing for an Audience of One means being content with doing "small things for God with great love."*

William Tyndale, burned at the stake for producing English translations of the Bible, once said, "There is no better job than another to please God: to pour water, to wash dishes, to be a cobbler, or an apostle. All is one, as touching the deed: to please God."[48] *Playing for an Audience of One means not envying the role that someone else might be playing in the Kingdom.*

Martin Luther King, Jr., said, "If a man is called to be a street sweeper, he should street-sweep even as Michelangelo painted, or Beethoven composed music....He should sweep streets so well that all the hosts of heaven and earth will pause to say, 'Here lived a great street sweeper who did his job well.'"[49] *Playing for an Audience of One means doing whatever it is you do with every ounce of passion and energy you've got.*

Brother Lawrence, the lord of all pots and pans, reminds us of our true vocation: "Our sole occupation in life is to please God."[50] *Playing for an Audience of One means resting in the conviction that your faithfulness to God is enough by which to live.*

Faithfulness Is the Real Barometer

Over the past several years, God's calling on my life has become crystallized to the point where I can summarize it in three words: "tell the Story." I am finally beginning to see what it means to be faithful to this calling. Whether I'm preaching a sermon, leading a Bible study, or engaging someone in a one-on-one conversation, God is simply calling me to tell His Story, and then trust that the telling of the Story has the power to change lives.

Here's the deeper lesson that I've needed to learn about myself over the past couple of years: *There is a tendency for me to confuse my calling 'to tell the Story' with my desire to see people respond (in a certain way) to my telling of the Story.* An entry from my prayer journal illustrates the struggle I so often feel:

Lord Jesus, I find myself again and again being tempted to focus my attention on the kind of response I get when I teach or preach. I know it's just an attempt to justify myself and validate the significance of my service. Help me to be identified and satisfied simply in telling the Story without the trappings of applause or respect, or any other response that I want to see—even conversions—which can cloud the way You want me to view myself and my calling.

I think many of us struggle at this very point: confusing what we're called to do with how people will respond to what we're doing. From there, we slip into evaluating our lives on the basis of other people's responses to what we're doing, instead of on the merits of being faithful to what God has called us to do.

Leighton Ford, in his book *Good News Is for Sharing*, tells the story of how a young pastor friend of his was used to lead an imprisoned, hardened criminal to Christ. This criminal, who became a Christian, told the pastor, "Now preacher, don't get a big head because I have accepted Christ. You are just the twenty-fifth man." On asking what that meant, the pastor was told that at least twenty-four others had shared with him about Christ and his conversion was the effect of all of these together.[51]

God continues to whisper to me: *Don't worry about the response. Whether you get to be the twenty-fifth man or not, just keep telling the Story.*

Moses eventually came to this same conviction about his calling. He had questioned God, cried out to Him in frustration and disappointment, and slipped into self- doubt about his speaking abilities. But in the end, Moses accepted rejection, loneliness, and failure (in the eyes of men) as part of the package deal of being faithful to God. Moses realized that faithfulness to God's calling was enough for which to live. One of the most striking verses in the Exodus story highlights the spiritual shift that took place in Moses:

"Moses ... did just as the Lord commanded."

—Ex. 7:6

Think about the significance of that simple statement. Everything Moses had experienced to this point in the story felt like failure. But on this day, Moses turned a corner in his relationship with God. He resolved to obey God regardless of what felt like failure, regardless of the rejection and loneliness he might continue to experience during the journey, and regardless of the pain and suffering he might cause others. On this day, Moses became free from measuring himself against anyone else's response other than the Lord's. It wouldn't be the last time Moses ever felt frustration or disappointment, but never again would he slip into self-doubt over the Hebrews' evaluation of his leadership. Moses was no longer locked into believing the lie that following God meant everything would play out the way he hoped.

Holiness or Happiness?

When you tell non-Christians that saying yes to Jesus will result in a happier, more successful life, you had better qualify what you mean. Otherwise you are selling unsuspecting people a bill of goods. I can't tell you how many Christians have come into my office because they deeply believed that either they had blown it or that God didn't care about them anymore. The primary problem in the majority of these cases was this: they could not reconcile what was happening in their lives with the version of the gospel they had signed on to.

Helmut Thielicke, a renowned author and theologian, was asked what he thought was the most significant flaw among American Christians. Without missing a beat, he replied, "They have an inadequate view of suffering....The worship of success is generally the form of idol worship which the devil cultivates most."[52]

Jesus' primary objective in our lives is not to make us *happy*, at least not the way most of us want to define happiness. His primary purpose is to make us *holy*. Not holier than thou. Not spiritually self-righteous. There are already way too many of those kinds of Christians out there. God is looking for people who will be holy: wholly belonging to Him. Abraham Kuyper points out why: "There is not one inch in the entire realm of life about which Christ, who is Sovereign of all, does not cry out, 'Mine!'"[53]

Happiness is part of God's eternal plan for us, but only in so far as it takes second place behind His desire for a holy people, a people who belong wholly to Him.

There Will Be a Target on Your Back

Here is where it gets exciting…and dangerous. When you fully surrender yourself to God, in a very real sense you are putting a target on your back. If you took the step of "throwing down your staff" at the end of the previous chapter, be forewarned: you're now a marked human being. Yes, God uses pain, suffering, and "failure" to shape us and move us along in the journey toward playing for an Audience of One. But lest I paint a distorted picture of God as the sole cosmic Player intersecting our lives, let me clarify. There is also an enemy of our souls who hates it when we give ourselves to God in a total and complete way; hates it when we sell out to follow Jesus regardless of the price tag. He flat out hates you.

Don't take it personally. The enemy's hatred is not directed toward you as much as it is a reflection of his hatred toward God. Ever since Satan lost the war with God, and was expelled from heaven and cast down to earth, he focuses his rage against human beings in retaliation against the One who defeated and shamed him:

> Then the dragon was enraged…and went off to make war against…those who obey God's commandments and hold to the testimony of Jesus.
>
> —Rev. 12:17

Satan seeks to get back at God by inflicting pain upon those who belong wholly to Him. This pain takes many forms. Loneliness, disappointment, and rejection are just a sampling that he used on Moses. Who do you think inspired the Hebrew slaves' rejection of Moses? Satan uses all kinds of apparent failure to discourage us to throw in the towel. He knows that when we surrender ourselves completely to God, we take our position on the frontlines of the spiritual battle. And this is where we pose a real threat to him. That's why Satan seeks to overwhelm us with our feelings of failure. He's hoping we'll go AWOL on our commitment to keep following God.

The enemy is not all that concerned about nominal Christians whose relationship with God is simply an arrangement for their sins to be forgiven. That kind of Christian doesn't cause him to lose any sleep. Why should he stay awake worrying about halfhearted believers who are no threat to take any of his territory? But like the evil Sauron in *The Lord of the Rings*, Satan fixes his eye upon those who have completely aligned themselves with the One he hates. That's why you should not be surprised when "the flaming arrows of the evil one" (Eph. 6:16) start whizzing past your head. There is a target on your back.

It might not sound very seeker sensitive, but we need to speak openly with seeking non-Christians about the reality of this target on our backs. Some hesitate to do so out of fear of scaring away potential converts. But when we let a marketing strategy dictate what part of the Story we tell people, we dishonor God and pervert the integrity of the message. We also do a disservice to those who end up responding to the gospel. Telling the truth about what they're up against prepares them for the reality in which they will live if they commit themselves to Christ.

Adam was a single dad who struggled with deep bouts of depression. He wandered aimlessly through most of his life. Then he said yes to Jesus. The depression didn't just "disappear." But the sense of meaninglessness that previously marked his life did begin to be transformed by the truth that God loved him and had a purpose for his life. A few months after receiving Christ, Adam and I began to talk about baptism. I told him how the Holy Spirit would continue to be right there to help him take this step. But I also warned him that baptism was a public declaration of his aligning himself with Jesus, and that there would be another who would be watching him, one who would seek to sabotage him early in his new journey with God.

With his eyes wide open to what he was doing, Adam got baptized that next Sunday. It was a glorious service. God's grace was palpable. There were friends of Adam's in church that morning who hadn't thought about God in a long time. You could see in their eyes a hunger for what Adam was experiencing. His testimony was clearly pointing other people to Jesus. Adam was on the frontlines, and God was using him!

And the enemy didn't like it. The next day, Adam called me from work. The first words out of his mouth were: "Thanks for warning me about the target on my back."

Adam had been fired that very morning. Except for his daughter, the only consistent and meaningful aspect of his life, prior to meeting Jesus, was his job. He had been a foreman in the company for eight years. His boss loved the work Adam did, but he hated Adam's new religion. The boss didn't keep his hatred a secret either. He knew about Adam's decision to be baptized, and his belittling words leading up to the event clearly communicated what he thought about it. When Adam walked onto the job site the next morning, just eighteen hours after publicly declaring his allegiance to Jesus, he was fired.

Despite being new to the faith, though, Adam was not shell-shocked. His eyes were wide open to what was going on. His commitment to Jesus wasn't based on any prosperity version of Christianity, the kind where pseudo-gospel peddlers write people checks that God never agreed to sign. Adam knew what was going on, and it actually encouraged him in his walk with God. As the saying goes, "Forewarned is forearmed." The setback actually provided him with an opportunity to learn something else about having a target on his back: *we need not fear this enemy of our souls*. God's love and provision are sufficient even amidst such attacks. Nothing and nobody can take us out of the game of life before God says it's time.

God Is Sovereign

If only we lived like we believed this to be true. Peace, joy, and a holy boldness would be ours as soon as we began to rest in the truth that there is nothing Satan can inflict upon us that has not gone first through the loving hands of our sovereign God. Our attitude would be like that of Julio Ruibal, who, despite constant threats on his life, proclaimed, "I am immortal until I have done everything God has for me to do!"[54]

Julio, known as the Apostle to the Andes, followed God's leading to Cali, Colombia, one of the leading cities in the Central American drug cartel. His vision of a spiritual revival inspired him to live his life with total abandonment to God. With it came a confidence that overruled all fear of pain and rejection. Julio's trust in God was not Pollyanna-driven, though. He knew the potential price tag of his obedience to God. In fact, just before his death, Julio shared with his wife two revelations given to him by God: first, that he sensed he was in mortal danger, and second, that the wellsprings of revival were about to break forth in Cali.

Days later, Pastor Julio was shot down in cold blood. He was martyred, but not a minute before he had done everything God had for him to do. The waves of revival began washing over the city of Cali at the time of his death. His funeral service catalyzed the pastors of the city to come together and forge a covenant of unity between them. In the weeks and months that followed Julio's death, literally thousands of people throughout Cali came to Christ.

The enemy cannot take us out before God grants him permission. There is nothing Satan can inflict upon us that has not first gone through the loving hands of our sovereign God. *We are immortal until we have done everything God has for us to do.*

Tertullian, a second century early church father, understood that apparent failure, and even death itself, could not stop God from advancing His Kingdom in the world. Here's what he said to the rulers of the Roman world, who were seeking to extinguish the Christian movement:

> Kill us, torture us, condemn us, grind us to the dust....The more you mow us down the more we grow; the seed (of the church) is the blood of the saints.[55]

We are immortal until we have done everything God has for us to do.

From the Hall of Shame to the Hall of Fame

Moses settled the failure issue. No longer was the pain and fear of rejection an obstacle to his obedience to God. It didn't matter what his fellow Hebrews thought of him. Instead, faithfulness to God became his spiritual trademark: Moses did just as the Lord commanded.

Moses kept swinging the bat, and his obedience to God eventually led to the accomplishment of the rescue mission. Not only that, but Moses even got a brief reprieve from the rejection of his fellow Hebrews after they crossed the Red Sea. The final verse of the Exodus story reads:

> When the Israelites saw the great power of the Lord displayed against the Egyptians, the people ... put their trust...in Moses.
>
> —Ex. 14:31

If only the Israelites' trust in Moses had lasted. Suffice it to say, it didn't. You know how long it was before "their trust" in him waned? Not long...

> *Three days later:* The people grumbled against Moses, saying, "What are we to drink?"
>
> —Ex. 15:24

> *One month later:* The whole community grumbled against Moses..."If only we had died by the Lord's hand in Egypt! There we sat around pots of meat and ate all the food we wanted, but you have brought us out into this desert to starve."
>
> —Ex. 16:2

> *For the next forty years:* Moses endured more grumbling, deeper loneliness, and further rejection by his fellow Hebrews.
>
> —Ex 16ff

You can see why the initial failures in Egypt were so important for Moses' spiritual maturity. Satan sought to destroy Moses with them, but God was using them to fashion a leader who would play for an Audience of One no matter the cost, no matter the rejection.

Ironically, it was only after Moses died that he achieved a standing of greatness among God's people. The Israelites didn't realize what they had in Moses until he was taken from them. "Often the crowd does not recognize a leader until he has gone, and then they build a monument for him with the stone they threw at him in life."[56]

Of course, Moses needed no monument to be built for him on earth. Upon his death, he was immediately inducted into the celestial Hall of Fame. He became a living and breathing monument in that eternal Cooperstown — just read the appropriately named "Hall of Faith" chapter of Hebrews 11. Moses is in there with the best of them. His life was marked with loneliness, rejection, and apparent failure, but his faithfulness to God over the long haul made him a first ballot shoo-in for the Hall. Because unlike Major League Baseball, where retired players must win a majority of votes from hundreds of sportswriters in order to get into the Hall of Fame, getting into the Hall of Faith is simply contingent on winning the approval of the only One whose vote counts: God. And Moses got His vote.

May you learn to accept "failure" as part of the journey toward being inducted into the eternal Hall of Faith, where you'll hear those words that will erase the pain of every apparent failure: *Well done, good and faithful servant. Enter into your rest.*

Prayer of a Faithful "Failure"

"Though You slay me, yet will I trust in You."

—Job (13:15)

Going Deeper

1. Are there past failures that still haunt you? Take some time to talk with God about them, even if you're still angry or frustrated. He can handle it.

2. Is there someone whose evaluation of you haunts your thinking? Ask God to do the kind of work He did in Moses to set you free from the tyranny of their opinions.

3. Are you ready to accept the truth that Jesus' primary purpose for your life is not to make you happy, but to make you holy? Tell someone about this new conviction.

4. Have you turned that corner in your relationship with God where you're willing to obey Him—even if it feels like failure? If so, in what area of your life will the marks of "failure" be the most difficult to deal with? Start talking to God about it now.

5. Are you living with the awareness that there is a target on your back? Find a way to remind yourself of this reality when things aren't going your way and you're tempted to go AWOL on your total commitment to Jesus.

6. Do you have Pastor Julio's perspective on life? Can you say with conviction, "I am immortal until I have done everything God has for me to do"? What might it start to look like for you to actually live with this kind of holy boldness?

Chapter 6

Playing Second Fiddle

If your vision is for a year, plant wheat.
If your vision is for ten years, plant trees.
If your vision is for a lifetime, plant people.
                            —Ancient Chinese Proverb

IF SOMEONE OFFERED to give you ten thousand dollars every day for a month, or start you out with a penny that would be doubled each day for thirty-one days, which would you choose?

Select Door #1, and the grand total is fairly easy to figure: $10,000 x 31 days = $310,000. Not bad.

What about Door #2? This one may require a calculator. Here's how it looks at the end of a week: $.01 x2 = $.02 x2 = $.04 x2 = $.08 x2 = $.16 x2 = $.32 x2 = $.64! After one week of daily doubling your initial penny, you have a whopping sixty-four cents! It doesn't look you'll be able to quit your day job. Perhaps you would like to go back to Door #1 and take the $310,000?

If you hold out for the law of multiplication to make up ground, though, you will be glad you did. By the end of the month, that penny with which you started out will become $10,737,418.24! (This is where most people feel the need to check my math. Go ahead and get out your calculator—it's an enlightening exercise!)

That's the difference between the law of addition and the law of multiplication: about ten million dollars. At first glance, it seems far more lucrative to choose a large lump sum of money each day. But over the long haul the law of multiplication more than catches and surpasses the law of addition. In fact, the gap between these two options grows exponentially with each passing day.

The Law of Multiplication in God's Kingdom

The law of multiplication is not only more productive in mathematics; it's more productive in the kingdom as well. That's why the apostle Paul poured himself into young leaders like Timothy, Titus, Silas, Epaphras, Tychicus, Aristarchus, Luke, Lydia, and others. Paul's Kingdom gains cannot be figured simply by *adding* up the number of his converts, but by calculating (if it's even possible) the *multiplied* impact he had on the world through his disciples. Paul poured his life into these apprentices, knowing they would influence others for Christ. And they did:

- Timothy became a fellow missionary, a church planter, and an apostolic representative among the Gentiles. He also became pastor of one of the most influential churches of the first century: Ephesus.
- Titus became a missionary and an apostolic representative in many of the more challenging Gentile churches, such as those in Corinth and Crete.
- Silas became an evangelist and church planter.
- Epaphras became pastor of the church in Colosse.
- Tychicus became an apostolic representative. His ministry was significant among the churches in the province of Asia, particularly those in Ephesus, Colosse, and Crete.
- Aristarchus became a missionary companion of Paul, as well as the "project manager" for getting the money raised by the Gentile churches to the needy believers in Jerusalem.
- Luke became a missionary companion of Paul to the far reaches of the Roman Empire, as well as the author of the third Gospel and the book of Acts.

- Lydia became the point person for the church in Philippi's base of operations.

Paul couldn't be in all of these places at the same time, but he could impact them for Christ through these men and women. Paul's influence through his ministry lieutenants literally reached across the Roman Empire, underscoring the power of the law of multiplication. No wonder he reminded Timothy to keep passing the baton to others:

> The things you have heard me say in the presence of many witnesses entrust to reliable men who will also be qualified to teach others.
>
> —2 Tim. 2:2

This is what you do if you want to see the law of multiplication continue to do its thing. Paul knew that when leaders reproduce themselves in the lives of young men and women, God's kingdom is more effectively advanced in the world. That's why he invested so much time in individuals. He knew if he poured himself into even one life, such that he reproduced his convictions, passions, and way of life in that person, the potential effect would be much greater than it might appear at first. After all, that one person can become a change agent in the life of another, who can become a change agent in the life of another, and so on. The ripple effect of this kind of discipleship model can take the world by storm. Paul took Timothy and others under his wing and poured his life into them, such that he could say to them:

> You…know all about my teaching, my way of life, my purpose, faith, patience, love, endurance.
>
> —2 Tim. 3:10

Paul didn't just dream up this multiplication ministry model. And it wasn't downloaded to him on the road to Damascus, either. Many Christians assume that the Damascus Road experience (all by itself) transformed Paul and prepared him to immediately take the gospel to the four corners of the globe—with a discipleship program already mapped out for him. That's not how it happened, though. Paul learned it. More accurately, it was modeled for him.

Who Passed the Baton to Paul?

Jesus did commission Paul to be the apostle to the Gentiles. But there was still one very significant problem facing Paul: the early church didn't want anything to do with him. He had been a persecutor of Christians. His hands were still stained with the blood of the first martyr, Stephen, when Jesus called him. Paul was the one who had authorized Stephen's stoning. The Jerusalem Church didn't want to extend the right hand of fellowship to Paul, much less the right hand of ministry:

> When (Paul) came to Jerusalem, he tried to join the disciples, but they were all afraid of him, not believing he really was a disciple.
>
> —Acts 9:26

It's tough to become the apostle to the Gentiles when the church refuses to acknowledge that you're even a Christian!

Imagine how tough this must have been for Paul. He so badly wanted to put the past behind him, and start using his gifts for Jesus. And yet the church was putting up an impenetrable wall of resistance. There didn't seem to be one Christian in all of Jerusalem who would give him the time of day. Everyone remembered Stephen. Nobody had forgotten that Paul had been the one who signed off on his execution. Paul didn't have a single inroad with anyone in the entire Jerusalem Church...*until Barnabas entered his life*:

> But Barnabas took (Paul) and brought him to the apostles.
>
> —Acts 9:27a

In my Bible, this word, "But," is circled, underlined, and highlighted. It sets up one of the most significant turning points in Paul's life and ministry. It didn't look like there was any way for Paul to get into the Jerusalem church or get a hearing with the apostles, *but* then Barnabas brought him to them.

Who was this Barnabas, that he could not only get Paul through the front door of the church, but into the inner circle of the apostles? Barnabas wasn't an apostle, a deacon, or a pastor. He didn't have an official title in the Jerusalem church. He did have influence and resources, though, and he used both for God. The book of Acts introduces Barnabas this way:

> Joseph, a Levite from Cyprus, whom the apostles called Barnabas (which means Son of Encouragement), sold a field he owned and brought the money and put it at the apostles' feet.
> —Acts 4:36-37

Putting his money "at the apostles' feet" was a symbol of Barnabas's willingness to put himself and his gifts under the leadership of the church. He was the epitome of a team player. In fact, "Barnabas," which means, "son of encouragement," was a nickname given to him because of his reputation as an encourager. His credibility among the early church leaders was high, particularly among the apostles. And Barnabas risked it all in order to take a chance on Paul.

Think of what Barnabas was laying on the line in order to bring Paul to the apostles. Besides risking his own credibility and reputation, Barnabas was also risking the wellbeing of the church. What if Barnabas was wrong about Paul? What if Paul's conversion was nothing more than a ploy to break into the inner circle of the church in order to find out who and where the leaders were? What if Barnabas was unknowingly leading the enemy straight into the leadership circle of the Jerusalem Church? Schemes like this happened in the first century. In some parts of the world today, where the church has had to go underground, they still happen. There's no way to spin it—Barnabas took a huge risk in bringing Paul to the apostles.

It's not that Barnabas threw all caution to the wind, though. He was a very discerning man. And he did his homework on Paul. Here's what Barnabas told the apostles he had discovered about Paul:

> He told them how Paul on his journey had seen the Lord and that the Lord had spoken to him, and how in Damascus he had preached fearlessly in the name of Jesus.
> —Acts 9:27b

Following Paul's alleged conversion to Christianity, Barnabas had researched his story to ensure it was legitimate. Barnabas found out Paul had been preaching fearlessly about Jesus in Damascus, risking his own

life in the process. As Barnabas took the time to examine the details of
Paul's story, he found signs of authenticity. His verdict: Paul was indeed
the genuine article. Once that question was settled in Barnabas's heart,
he not only helped get Paul through the front door of the church, he
also got him off the sidelines and into the ministry game:

> So Paul stayed with them and moved about freely in Jerusalem,
> speaking boldly in the name of the Lord.
>
> —Acts 9:28

No Lone Rangers

Soon after Paul began preaching the gospel in Jerusalem, he found
himself in trouble with the Jewish community. This time around,
though, the believers in Jerusalem went from ostracizing Paul to rescuing
him from danger:

> Paul talked and debated with the Grecian Jews, but they tried to
> kill him. When the brothers learned of this they took him down to
> Caesarea and sent him off to Tarsus.
>
> —Acts 9:30

If it weren't for Barnabas's endorsement of Paul, the Jerusalem
Christians never would have lifted a finger to save him. Paul would
have been dead before he had an opportunity to preach the gospel to
a single Gentile, much less become their apostle! But the believers in
Jerusalem followed Barnabas's lead by risking their own necks to get Paul
out of town safely. As soon as they found out about the death threat,
they smuggled him out of the city and sent him back to his hometown
of Tarsus.

Sometimes Christians picture Paul as being a spiritual superhero, a
lone ranger who never needed anybody's help to fulfill God's call on his
life. At best this is a caricature of Paul. There were certainly points when
Paul stood alone, when he needed to obey God "though none would go
with him." But there were other moments in his life when he desperately
needed people like Barnabas to stand in the gap for him. Paul never
would have fulfilled Christ's calling on his life without Barnabas.

If the Damascus Road experience was the *event* that most impacted Paul, then Barnabas was the *person* who most impacted him. If it weren't for Barnabas, Paul never would have been able to get into the Jerusalem church to show the apostles the genuineness of his faith. If it weren't for Barnabas, Paul never would have been able to get out of Jerusalem when his life was in jeopardy. Barnabas not only saved Paul's life, he brought him into a larger church family, introduced him to people in leadership, and gave him an opportunity to preach the gospel in the very city where he previously had been known as a persecutor of the faith.

And this was just the beginning of Barnabas' influence on Paul's life.

From Obscurity to the Frontlines

Years later, while Paul was still in Tarsus, a revival broke out in the city of Antioch. This particular revival was significant because it was the first time large numbers of Gentiles had ever come to faith in Christ. Not only that, but this revival was happening without an apostle or an officially endorsed missionary from Jerusalem leading the charge. It was simply the result of persecuted Christians being scattered all over the Roman Empire, and sharing the gospel wherever they went. So the apostles decided they had better send someone they trusted to Antioch to check out this leader-less revival to make sure it was legitimate. Their choice was Barnabas, which further underscores the kind of respect he had among the apostles. Notice what Barnabas did once he got to Antioch:

> When Barnabas arrived and saw the evidence of the grace of God, he was glad and encouraged them all to remain true to the Lord with all their hearts. He was a good man, full of the Holy Spirit and faith, and a great number of people were brought to the Lord.
>
> —Acts 11:23-24

The first thing Barnabas did when he got to Antioch was look for signs of authenticity, what Luke calls "evidence of the grace of God." Barnabas was a man of great spiritual discernment. He already had demonstrated this gift to the apostles in his relationship with Paul. It's no wonder the apostles sent Barnabas to Antioch. The church needed someone with wisdom to assess the situation. It didn't take Barnabas long to conclude that the Antioch Gentiles' faith was genuine. So Barnabas started doing what came natural to him: encouraging them all to remain true to the Lord with all their hearts.

Meanwhile, Paul was still back in Tarsus.

Barnabas was having a blast building up the new fledgling fellowship in Antioch. Gentiles were being saved, new Christians were being discipled, and the church was growing. That's when Barnabas remembered Paul, the persecutor turned preacher, whom Jesus had called to be the apostle to the Gentiles. Barnabas knew Paul's story. He knew the call on Paul's life. He also knew Paul should be there in Antioch, helping fan into flame the work that the Holy Spirit was doing among the Gentiles. So Barnabas took what ended up being one of the most kingdom-significant steps of his life:

> Then Barnabas went to Tarsus to look for Paul.
>
> —Acts 11:25

It actually required quite a few "steps" for Barnabas to get to Paul. Tarsus was over a hundred miles from Antioch. That's how badly Barnabas wanted to recruit Paul to join him in ministering to the Gentiles. When Barnabas found him, he invited him back into the game. After having spent years in relative obscurity, Paul didn't need to be asked twice:

> For a whole year Barnabas and Paul met with the church and taught great numbers of people. The disciples were called Christians first at Antioch.
>
> —Acts 11:26

Doing Two Things Simultaneously

The Antioch church had the privilege of growing up under the one-two teaching punch of Barnabas and Paul. Perhaps more importantly for the future of the Jesus movement, Paul had the privilege of growing up under the encouragement and example of Barnabas. There is nothing quite like being able to serve side by side in the trenches with a coach or mentor who believes in you, and who gives you the opportunity to do something that counts for God's kingdom. Barnabas was doing two things simultaneously during that year in Antioch:

1. He was overseeing *the mission*: teaching and discipling the Gentile believers in Antioch, and giving critical leadership to this fledgling church.
2. He was mentoring *the man*: creating a space on the team for Paul to teach and lead, giving him a real kingdom role to play, and cheering him on as he did it.

Sometimes in the church we get tunnel vision on the conversion aspect of the harvest. We forget about the long-term investment of mentoring younger potential leaders. It's understandable. We need to have a sense of urgency about seeing souls saved. But the desire to produce a harvest *now* should not be at the expense of raising up leaders who can multiply the effort needed *later*. If we are truly concerned about the harvest, then we must take the time to pour ourselves into people's lives:

> If your vision is for a year, plant wheat.
> If your vision is for ten years, plant trees.
> If your vision is for a lifetime, plant people.

Like Barnabas, we must do two things simultaneously.

Carolyn's life and vision for the kingdom was radically impacted because someone in our church took the time to play a Barnabas role in her life:

> Looking back at the relationship I had with my mentor, I can see how critical it was to my growth as a Christian. Not just because I learned how to lead a Bible study for junior-high students, or preach a sermon, or identify my spiritual gifts. What was most significant about my mentoring relationship was the trust that I experienced. I had someone with whom I could talk about personal struggles, someone whom I trusted to give me godly advice. This mentoring relationship

was so important to me because it gave me an opportunity each week, sometimes for only an hour or so, to connect with someone who was passionate about following Jesus. Maybe 1 hour out of 168 hours each week doesn't sound like enough time to really influence someone's life, but I know from experience that it is more than enough time. It was the only time each week when I could open up and honestly talk with someone. Countless times I would be on the verge of giving up on my faith due to being plagued by doubts, overwhelmed by my own legalism, or just plain because I preferred to disobey God. And yet I would wait to make that final decision to abandon Christianity until Wednesday rolled around and I could talk with my mentor about whatever was eating at me. I can say fairly certainly that without having been in a mentoring relationship I would have either lost my faith completely, or I would have become one of those Sunday Christians who might as well be an atheist the other six days of the week. It's not that my mentor had all of the answers. At times, simply listening was what really mattered most. By showing Christ's love to me in these ways, it allowed me to mature into a stronger Christian — to the point where I can now think about pouring myself into someone who is newer in the faith.

It's just not enough for local churches to pursue making disciples through preaching and programs alone. We must share our *lives* with people as well. We need to learn to do two things simultaneously. Barnabas modeled that for Paul. In fact, his example deeply influenced the way Paul would do ministry for the rest of his life. Paul's words to the Thessalonians years later clearly illustrates his relational ministry philosophy:

> We loved you so much that we were delighted to share with you not only the gospel of God *but our lives as well.*
>
> —1 Thess. 2:8, emphasis mine

Passing the Leadership Baton

After a year of teaching together in Antioch, Barnabas and Paul were set apart by the Holy Spirit for another ministry assignment. They would continue to serve together, but this time they would take the gospel to three more groups of Gentiles in other parts of the Roman

Empire. The Antioch church commissioned Barnabas and Paul in that order. In fact, between Acts 11:26–13:13, the narrative always mentions Barnabas first as a way of designating he was the leader of the team. First Barnabas, then Paul.

Then, in the middle of their missionary journey to the Gentiles, without any fanfare, Barnabas passed the leadership baton to Paul. From that time on, with the exception of when they were back in Jerusalem (Barnabas's stomping grounds) at the church council (Acts 15), the narrative always reads: "Paul and Barnabas." This was Luke's not-so-subtle way of highlighting that Paul had become the leader of the team.

Here's the amazing thing: Barnabas didn't have an ego trip over the leadership change. He didn't try and hold onto his position as a way of shoring up his self-worth or his value to the church. The leadership transition didn't happen because of a hostile takeover, a church split, or an ultimatum. The baton got passed because Barnabas was secure enough to acknowledge that there was somebody else who needed to be taking the lead. Barnabas was a big enough man to let Paul, whom Jesus had called to become the apostle to the Gentiles, be the point person. As their missionary journey took them deeper into Gentile territory, it just made sense that Paul should take the lead. Barnabas knew it was time to take a step back, and so he did.

Barnabas not only relinquished the reins as the point person, he stayed on the team. Most of the time when leaders come to the conviction that there is someone better suited or gifted to play a role they have been playing, they either tighten their grip on the leadership position or they leave the team altogether to serve elsewhere. Depending on the circumstances surrounding the transition, it might be necessary for the senior leader to move on. Often times, though, the new leader simply loses out on the wisdom and encouragement that could be given by the previous leader who is passing the baton.

Barnabas stayed on board and closed the loop for how to help younger leaders reach their full serving potential:

I serve, you watch me.

I serve, you serve with me.

You serve, I serve with you.
You serve, I watch you.

Checking Our Ego at the Door

For those of us who find ourselves playing a leadership role, these last two steps are sometimes the most difficult because they kick against our pride and ego. We might secretly wonder: *What if people think I'm not leading anymore because I burned out, or because I couldn't handle the pressure? What if I don't feel needed or important to the team anymore? What will people think if my replacement ends up doing a better job than me? Do I really want to hang around to hear about it?*

Barnabas could have let his mind drift to questions like these, but he didn't.

A word of warning to those of you who "need" to be needed: a spirit of indispensability will choke the life out of an organization, and poison the purity of your service. The antidote for "needing" to be indispensable is to invite others into the game with you, give them an opportunity to serve in a real and meaningful way, and then coach and encourage them on to fruitfulness. Not only will this be good for the kingdom, and build a healthier base of servant-leaders within your church, it will be good for your own soul, too. It will purify your motives and remind you that true service is done for an Audience of One.

Because Barnabas's identity was wrapped up in Christ, he was willing to play whatever role in the kingdom he needed to play—even if that meant relinquishing the leadership reins. He didn't view his new role on the team as a demotion. He wasn't playing for positions, power, titles, or trophies. Barnabas was content to be cast as a supporting actor if that's what was best for the kingdom of God. His gifts were surrendered to God; they were at His disposal. If God wanted him to lead the charge, he was willing. If God wanted him to play a "behind the scenes" role, then that was fine, too. Barnabas wasn't going to cling to his leadership position as though it was what gave meaning and significance to his life. Barnabas knew who he was. He was "the son of encouragement." And he could stay true to that calling regardless of where God placed him.

The willingness to put ego and personal ambition on the back burner is a distinguishing mark of those who truly play for an Audience of One. Leonard Bernstein, the composer and conductor of the New York Philharmonic, was once asked what he thought was the most difficult instrument in the orchestra to play. Without missing a beat, he responded, "Second fiddle!"[57] Nobody watches the second fiddler. Everyone's eyes are on the person playing the first violin. But if the second fiddler doesn't play her part well, it makes the lead instrument look (and sound) very bad. On the other hand, by playing well, the second fiddler has the capacity to make the first fiddler look (and sound) very good. As the old saying goes, "It takes more grace than I can tell to play the second fiddle well."

A close cousin of "failing" for God is being able to "play the second fiddle." Second fiddlers are at a premium these days. They do far more for the kingdom than first meets the eye because the nature of their service is frequently behind the scenes. The value of second fiddlers is underestimated because they typically make the lead instruments sound better. Consequently, the applause and credit usually goes to the point people. Second fiddlers who can stomach this are invaluable to the work of the kingdom. Maybe that's why God's blessing and anointing flows toward those who are willing to play second fiddle well.

Who Cares Who Gets the Glory!

I will never forget God's nearly audible voice whispering this truth to me. I had just finished graduate school and was on a plane to Seattle, where I was to begin serving in an associate pastor role. Prior to attending seminary, I had it in my mind that upon graduation I would serve in a senior pastor position somewhere. But God had other plans. During that flight to Seattle, I kept sensing God say to me, "There is nothing I can't do through someone who is unconcerned with who gets the glory." Over and over again during that five-hour flight, I heard those words until they became imprinted on my heart.

For the next seven years, my role as an associate pastor afforded me the incredible opportunity to bless, encourage, and support my senior pastor. Even when we disagreed (behind closed doors), I had the chance to embody a spirit of unity that became contagious to the rest of the church. Despite the fact that our congregation knew there were differences of opinion between the senior pastor and me, they frequently commented on the team spirit that existed between us. This kind of unity among the leadership has a way of "infecting" the rest of the congregation. And those who play a second fiddle role have the unique opportunity of leading the way in making God-honoring unity a reality in a local church, or any organization for that matter.

Playing second fiddle also brings with it temptation, though. There were times when I was tempted to give commentary on a ministry win in such a way that it highlighted my name on the church marquee. I know that when I gave into these temptations, it negatively affected the spiritual health of our church—even if nobody else detected what I was doing. Fortunately, God has been gracious with me when I've been inclined to go this way. I couldn't go very far down that road before I remembered the words He said to me during that plane flight: "There is nothing I can't do through someone who is unconcerned with who gets the glory."

The second fiddle principle is critical to recognize, regardless of the role you play in your church, workplace, or community. The fact of the matter is that every one plays second fiddle to someone. And even if you happen to be the leader, you still need to keep this second fiddle perspective in mind. Even the President of the United States, Ronald Reagan, used to keep a plaque on his desk at the Oval Office that read: "There is no limit to what a man can do or where he can go if he doesn't mind who gets the credit."

The temptation for so many of us is to buy into the lie that more power or a higher position or a bigger platform always translates into greater ministry potential. The economy of God does not necessarily work this way, though, particularly when those who are gifted spend so much of their time jockeying for the pole position. As Oswald Sanders writes:

> Many who aspire to leadership fail because they have never learned to follow. They are like boys playing war in the street, but all is quiet. When you ask, "Is there a truce?" they respond, "No, we are all generals. No one will obey the command to charge."[58]

The cause of Christ would be well served if there were a few more followers of Jesus willing to use their gifts to help others achieve kingdom victories. After all, if it's a win for the kingdom, who cares who gets the credit? Perhaps this is one of the reasons the American version of Christianity is so stagnant. There's a lack of second fiddle humility:

> The spiritual leader of today is the one who gladly works as an assistant and associate, humbly helping another achieve great things. Robert Morrison…wrote: "The great fault, I think, in our missions is that no one likes to be second."[59]

Why Barnabas and Paul Went Their Separate Ways

It would be incomplete to talk about Paul and Barnabas's relationship without mentioning the dispute that compelled them to go their separate ways. Their disagreement was over whether to invite John Mark to join them on their next mission trip. Mark had deserted them on their first missionary journey, turning tail and sailing back to Jerusalem. In doing so, he left Barnabas and Paul to complete the Gentile mission short-handed. Barnabas wanted to give Mark another chance. Paul would not even consider it.

Paul had good reasons for his hesitancy. The mission field was tough enough without having to deal with a team member bailing. Desertion was a serious offense. It was forgivable, but Paul wasn't willing to concede that Mark should get another chance to be back on the team. In his eyes, the stakes of the mission were too high to risk giving Mark another opportunity. Barnabas, on the other hand, was more than willing to take that risk.

Barnabas and Paul found themselves at an impasse. Which was more important to the kingdom of God: the mission or the man? I'm not sure either of them was necessarily wrong in his convictions. Luke, the author of the book of Acts and Paul's companion for much of his missionary career, doesn't take sides in his narrative. He simply writes:

> They had such a sharp disagreement that they parted company. Barnabas took Mark and sailed for Cyprus, but Paul chose Silas.
>
> —Acts 15:39-40

In the end, Barnabas couldn't give up on Mark. So just like he had done earlier with Paul, Barnabas took Mark under his wing. Again,

Barnabas risked his credibility, his time and energy, and even the success of the mission—in order to give Mark another chance. Despite all of the logical reasons why Barnabas shouldn't have wasted any more resources on Mark, he couldn't help himself. The one non-negotiable in Barnabas's life was that he remained true to who God made him to be: the son of encouragement. Barnabas played for an Audience of One, whether that meant being "demoted" to playing second fiddle, or taking relational risks that seemed foolhardy to everyone looking on from the outside.

A Multiplied Investment for the Kingdom

Barnabas's risk paid off. In fact, John Mark grew so much spiritually, and became such an asset to the kingdom, that by the end of Paul's life, Paul made this request of Timothy:

> Bring Mark with you, because he is helpful to me in my ministry.
>
> —2 Tim. 4:11

Paul never would have written those words about Mark except that Barnabas had been willing to give him another chance. Barnabas knew (like he had known with Paul) that God wanted to do something special through Mark.

About twenty years after Mark had deserted Barnabas and Paul in the middle of that first Gentile mission, Mark penned what became the second gospel in our New Testament. Not only did Mark write the gospel that bears his name, most biblical scholars agree his gospel was the primary source used by Matthew and Luke. In fact, 97 percent of Mark's gospel is found within Matthew's version, and 88 percent of it is found within the pages of Luke's narrative. In other words, three out of the four gospel accounts have John Mark's influence stamped upon them. This means that between Paul's thirteen letters and John Mark's gospel (and his ensuing influence on two of the other gospel accounts), these two men ended up being largely responsible for sixteen of the twenty-seven letters of the New Testament. Talk about kingdom significance!

This is another illustration of the law of multiplication at work. After all, both of these kingdom influencers (Paul and Mark) stood on the shoulders of another: *Barnabas*. Barnabas was willing to play the role of an encourager, behind the scenes if necessary, and even second fiddle if that was best for God's kingdom. Through his relationship with these two men, Barnabas, who didn't write even a single verse of Scripture, had his character, heart, and walk with Jesus imprinted all over the pages of two-thirds of the New Testament. *There is nothing God can't do through someone who is unconcerned with who gets the glory!*

Paul was the apostle to the Gentiles. He was the church planter in the key metropolitan cities of the Roman Empire. He was the disciple-maker and leadership developer of significant church leaders like Timothy, Titus, Silas, Epaphras, Tychicus, Aristarchus, and scores of others. He was the author of half of the New Testament. But his influence never would have been what it was without Barnabas's support, encouragement, and recruitment. Barnabas's willingness to put his ego on the back burner and pass the baton to Paul was his finest hour, both in terms of his ministry example and what it meant for the kingdom.

So much of Barnabas's influence came as a result of his willingness to play second fiddle. Like the seemingly insignificant penny at the beginning of this chapter, Barnabas's ministry wasn't flashy or attention-getting at first. His résumé wasn't filled with impressive sounding titles or positions. There were other positional leaders in the church whose ministries of addition, at first glance, seemed far more significant. But the transformational power of the Holy Spirit was working through Barnabas, doubling and redoubling his discipleship efforts and, over time, revealing the superiority of the law of multiplication.

You don't have to be the leader, teacher, boss, or one in charge of a ministry to make a difference for the kingdom of God. It may be that you are uniquely positioned to do something for God precisely in those places where you are serving in a behind-the-scenes capacity. Do not make the mistake of thinking only pastors or ministry leaders can be used to do great things for the kingdom. There is nothing God can't do through someone who is unconcerned with who gets the glory:

- Mothers, if you're feeling like you're on a meaningless treadmill of diapers, dishes, and dinners, remember: your second fiddle role is essential to the orchestra. The statistics don't lie. The most telling variable in the equation of whether or not children grow up to follow Christ is what happens within the four walls of their homes. Pour yourself into your children. Don't underestimate your second fiddle role. Think about the multiplying effect that raising your children in the Lord will have three or four generations from now!

- Assistants and associates, if you're feeling like you won't really contribute in a significant way until you're the one leading, remember: your second fiddle role is essential to the orchestra. Organizations and local churches crumble without second fiddlers who know how to put their egos and ambitions on the back burner for the good of the whole. You are strategically positioned *now* to support the point person, encourage the rest of the team, and create an environment within the organization that can become positively infected with a sense of unity.

- Laypeople, if you feel like you're a second-class Christian because you don't have an official leadership title at church, remember: your second fiddle role is essential to the orchestra. Go behind the scenes to make a difference. Send a note to your pastor. Take a Sunday to be a "one-person thank-you machine," expressing appreciation to everyone you see serving in the church: ushers, Sunday school teachers, nursery workers, etc. Don't underestimate the power of an encouraging word.

- Youth and children's workers, if you feel like the physical and emotional drain that comes from working with young people isn't producing anything for the kingdom, remember: your second fiddle role is essential to the orchestra. Keep pouring yourself into young people. Continue to teach them the Word. Encourage them with notes and words of affirmation. Invite them into your home. Pray for them. Recruit them to serve with you, where they can do something for God, while you mentor them at the same time.

Whether it's in your workplace, family, neighborhood, or local church, there is nothing God can't do through someone who is unconcerned with who gets the glory. Don't disqualify yourself because you lack position, speaking abilities, or higher education. God doesn't need any of those things to work mightily through someone. Howard Hendricks, the esteemed professor, prolific author, and brilliant theologian talked about the person who was the greatest influence on his life:

> I was born into a broken home in the city of Philadelphia. My parents were separated before I was born. I never saw them together except once in my life: when I was called to testify in a divorce court in the city of Philadelphia. And I'm sure that I could have been born, reared, died, gone to hell, and nobody would have particularly cared, except a small group of believers who got together in my neighborhood to found an evangelical church, and that was a miracle because everybody said, "You can't found an evangelical church in that community." You know, whenever somebody says, "You can't do it," I often think I hear God roar, "Oh really? Watch me!"
>
> That small group of individuals met to worship, and to study, and to develop a passion for that community. A man by the name of Walt came to the Sunday school superintendent and said, "I want to teach a Sunday school class."
>
> They said, "Wonderful, Walt, but we don't have any boys. You go out into the community, and anybody you pick up, that's your class."
>
> Walt came out. I'll never forget the day I met him. He was six feet, four inches tall. He said to me, as a little kid, "Hey, son, how would you like to go to Sunday school?" Well, anything that had "school" in it had to be a bad news item! And then he said, "How would you like to play marbles?" Oh! That was different! Would you believe we got down and played marbles till he beat me in every single game. I lost my marbles early in life. And by the time he got through, I didn't care where he was going, that's where I wanted to go.
>
> For your information, he picked up thirteen of us boys, nine of us from broken homes. Today, all thirteen of us are in full-time vocational Christian work.
>
> And Walt never went beyond sixth grade.[60]

Imagine what those thirteen men are accomplishing today for the kingdom of God! And they all stood on the shoulders of a very unlikely candidate: *Walt.*

What if Walt had disqualified himself because he wasn't smart enough? What if Walt had decided to let the "first fiddle" trained professionals, who lead church each Sunday morning, do it all? Thirteen men are serving Christ in full-time vocational ministry because of Walt. But it's not just that he affected the lives of thirteen boys. That by itself would be a worthy kingdom investment. Walt's life is actually impacting thousands of other people through those thirteen boys, and that's just in the first generation.

It's amazing what can happen through a penny, a Barnabas, or a Walt when the law of multiplication is at work—no matter how insignificant it looks at first. After all, God can do anything through someone who is willing to play the second fiddle!

Prayer of a Second Fiddler

"Let me decrease; let Him increase."

—John the Baptist (John 3:30)

Going Deeper

1. Where are you playing a second fiddle role? Who are the people "above you" whom you can help succeed, knowing this will be good for the organization, the team, the local church, and your own relationship with God?
2. In what ways is playing second fiddle difficult for your ego? Spend some time relinquishing your ambition and pride in order to get your "instrument" in tune with the Orchestra Conductor.
3. If you are in a leadership role, ask God to give your church, ministry, or organization second fiddlers who will follow in Barnabas's footsteps as they serve with you.
4. In what specific way could you build up a coworker or colleague in the eyes of your leader/supervisor? Do it, believing God will take care of you and your reputation.
5. Teach a children's Sunday school class or get involved in the lives of some youth. Look for ways to encourage them and pour your life into them. It doesn't take a seminary degree. Marbles did the trick for Walt!

Chapter 7

Even Jesus Said No

"Each of us has the time to do the whole will of God for our lives."[61]

—Oswald Sanders

HAVE YOU EVER noticed how frequently we tell each other how busy we are? Think about how often you respond to the question: "how are you?" with some form of "really busy." It got me wondering: are we all really that busy?

The U.S. Department of Labor did a study in 2006 to assess how Americans spend their time. Interestingly, as busy as we all seem to be, we still have quite a bit of discretionary time. In fact, 96 percent of those age fifteen and over have some form of leisure time *every day*. More surprising was the average amount of leisure time the study said each American has: over five hours a day![62]

Maybe you and I are hanging around the 4 percent of the population who do not have a minute to spare, but I doubt it. My guess is the "I'm busy" response is a badge some of us wear to portray an image of importance to each other. Maybe not consciously—some of us play the "I'm busy" card out of habit. But a lot of times, the motive lurking behind the "I'm busy" response is this: *important people are busy people; therefore, if others view me as busy, they'll also view me as important.*

Nobody Wants to Appear Lazy

Walk onto a university campus and nearly everyone is wearing this busy badge. Ironically, do you know who has the most free time, according to the same study? *Those between the ages of fifteen and twenty-four!*

I shouldn't be too hard on college students. I remember the pressure of finding sufficient time to study while working enough hours to pay for school. There was finals week, the stress of which major to choose, and figuring out what I wanted to be when I "grew up." On the other hand, I also remember playing cards all night and spending large chunks of time carrying out the perfect prank. For the most part, college was one of the most stress-free seasons of my life. If you heard us college students talk about our schedules, though, you would have thought we didn't have a minute to spare. There were some of us who truly were busy. Smitten with newfound independence from parents and having the freedom to do whatever we wanted whenever we wanted, there were some of us who filled our days with way too many things. But most of us just wanted to *sound* busy. After all, nobody wanted to be perceived as being lazy.

I recall one particular lunchtime conversation at college. (Note: lunch was the meal when a few of my floor mates finally dragged themselves out of bed!). The bags under their eyes compelled someone at the table to ask how they were doing. My buddies proceeded to report how insanely busy that day was going to be. They wondered aloud how they were going to get everything done. The air was thick with their anxiety and the busy-ness of their lives. I remember almost laughing at their sob story because I knew the reason for their fatigue and the ensuing busy-ness of that day. They had just pulled an all-nighter—not because they were studying for an exam or writing a paper, or working the graveyard shift. *They had stayed up all night attempting to conquer their latest video game.*

They conveniently edited out that part of the story!

After this lunchtime epiphany, I began to notice how, in my own subtle way, I did the same thing. I started to catch myself talking to people about how busy I was. Sometimes my words drifted that way out of habit. But other times, when I inspected the motive behind my words, I realized I did it, in part, because I didn't want people to view me as lazy. And since being perceived as lazy was a fate worse than death, I decided it was better to err on the side of sounding really busy. After all, I don't remember anyone ever responding to "how are you?" with: *You know, I don't have too much on my plate right now. There aren't too many responsibilities calling for my attention. I've figured out that a few hours of studying each evening really is adequate for keeping me on course with my professors' expectations. I've been getting plenty of sleep lately, too. I'm actually feeling quite rested these days. In fact, I've come to the realization that there really is sufficient time for me to do the whole will of God.* (I probably would have passed out from shock if someone had ever said that to me!)

I sensed God's Spirit asking me why I wanted to present such a "busy" image to others. The only reason I could come up with was that I was attempting to look important. I was not content with my schedule being approved by the Audience of One. I wanted it to be endorsed by my peers. I wanted to make sure that people saw what I did in the best light, so I shaded the description of my days in order to cast a longer shadow on the number of important things in my schedule—of course, eliminating any references to watching television or other "frivolous" activities.

God began to check me for portraying myself as being busy. I countered with, *But, God, what if I really am busy?*

The Spirit's next move put me in checkmate: "If you are finding yourself consistently being busy, you need to deal with it, not flaunt it."

God's voice was unmistakably clear: perpetual busy-ness isn't something to take pride in, or a badge to show off to our peers, or an excuse to justify a frenzied lifestyle, or the hand that Fate has dealt us. Busy-ness is a choice we make.

Was Jesus Busy?

There are seasons when life gets legitimately busy: the arrival of a new baby, a job challenge that needs extra attention, caring for a family member who is in crisis. There are other times when we inadvertently over-commit ourselves because we didn't realize how much time would be required to take on an additional responsibility. But frenetically paced days and margin-less schedules should be the exception, not the rule for life.

After all, Jesus was never "so busy." His days weren't run at break-neck speed. His life and ministry were full, but he was never frantically trying to figure out how to accomplish everything that needed to get done. People were impressed with many things about Jesus: the authority of His teaching, His ability to perform miracles, the compassion He showed for the poor, and His willingness to mingle with those on the margins of society. But not once in any of the Gospel accounts does anyone ever comment on how busy Jesus was getting His laundry list of ministry tasks checked off. Oswald Sanders writes:

> Our Lord...moved through life with measured steps, never hurried, though always surrounded by demands and crowds. When a person approached Him for help, Jesus gave the impression that He had no more important concern than the needs of His visitor.[63]

So why do most of us look so very different from Jesus when it comes to the pace and schedule of our lives? I've heard some folks argue that it's because Jesus didn't face the same kind of time challenges that we deal with today. Just for fun, let's consider a few of them:

- Jesus didn't have to fight against television, the Internet, or other modern day distractions that swallow up our time, right? (No, but He did live in an era where there were not only fewer technological advances, there was also no electricity. This meant when the sun went down, so did He. Jesus actually had fewer "working hours" each day to accomplish His mission!)
- Jesus didn't have to face the kind of bumper-to-bumper commutes we deal with, right? (No, but He did have to walk everywhere He went. His average speed: a "slightly slower than Autobahn" speed of 3 mph!)
- Jesus didn't have a wife or family responsibilities dividing His attention, right? (No, but He did have the burdens of an entire world resting on His shoulders. Specifically, He had the task of raising and training a dozen disciples who would lead His church when He was gone!)

The distinction between first and twenty-first century life doesn't really get at the difference between Jesus' schedule and ours. Just like us, Jesus had twenty-four hours a day to accomplish the Father's will for His life. The real reason He could live each day without ever feeling frantic about what He needed to get done was this: *Jesus always said yes to God's best and then no to the rest.*

Our lives are most significantly shaped by the way we use those two little words: *yes* and *no*. The real challenge is to learn to say yes to God's best, and then no to the rest. It's not complicated, but neither is it easy. Saying no is not just a matter of avoiding blatant sins, either. We also need to say no to good people and worthy causes when they compete with God's best for our time. If Satan can't get us to sin, he will try to keep us so busy going in a thousand different directions that we become distracted and divided from the most important things to which we should be giving our time.

Why Is *No* So Difficult?

The reason that perpetual busy-ness doesn't get addressed in our lives is we don't know how, aren't willing, or don't want to say no to the opportunities and invitations that come knocking on our door. This is particularly the case when they come from good people, inviting us to do good things for a good cause.

There's a story of a lighthouse keeper who was given just enough oil for one month, and charged with a single responsibility: keep the light burning every night. One day a woman came knocking on the door of the lighthouse, asking for oil so her children could stay warm. The lighthouse keeper was moved by her situation and obliged her plea. The next day, a farmer came with a similar request: his son needed oil for a lamp in order to do his homework. The lighthouse keeper still had oil, so he gave him a bit of it. Other townspeople caught wind of the lighthouse keeper's generosity, and came with their requests as well. The keeper saw each as a worthy request and measured out just enough oil to satisfy everyone. Near the end of the month, though, the tank in the lighthouse ran dry. That night the beacon was dark and three ships crashed on the rocks. Many lives were lost. When a government official investigated, the lighthouse keeper explained what he had done and why.

"You were given one task alone," insisted the official. "It was to keep the light burning. Everything else was secondary. There is no defense."

Many of us stretch ourselves thin because we don't want to disappoint people by saying no. Over the course of my life, I've been especially susceptible to requests when they are prefaced with, "But *nobody* else will do it" or "There isn't anyone who can do it as *well* as you." Saying yes on these occasions has given me an immediate sense of importance. It's also shielded me from the temporary pain of letting someone down or feeling guilty about saying no. Brennan Manning writes, "Because of our suffocating need to please others, we cannot say no with the same confidence with which we say yes. And so we overextend ourselves in people, projects, and causes, motivated not by personal commitment but by the fear of not living up to others' expectations."[64]

Few things are as draining as service that's driven by the desire to gain the approval of others. Craving the affection of others or fearing their disappointment entices us to cram the wrong things into our schedules. Perhaps you know what it is to commit to doing something, only to experience buyer's remorse once you have to live with that decision. You promise yourself that next time you'll say no. But when next time comes around, the pain of saying no to the person asking you seems greater than the fatigue you'll feel if you say yes. So you just say yes again. The personal mission statement at the top of some of our day-timers reads: *Becoming all things to all people—so that everyone might be pleased with me.*

Meanwhile, those specific things to which you know God has called you get the dregs of your time, energy, and attention. This is why learning to say no to good people and good causes may be one of the most important steps you take on the journey toward playing for an Audience of One.

You may find it difficult to say no because you don't want to miss out on anything that might be exciting or meaningful. The thought that others might have fun, experience something memorable, or serve in some kingdom-significant way without you feels unbearable. So you hedge your bets and try to do it all. We live in a culture that is committed to keeping our options open. "The condition we find ourselves in," says philosopher Dallas Willard, "can best be described as one of 'entanglement.' By contrast, the condition we must move to is that of single-minded focus upon doing the will of God in everything, distracted by nothing."[65]

Unfortunately, most of us prefer entanglement to feeling like we might miss out.

An even more likely reason we don't say no is we'd rather be over-committed than feel guilty. Somewhere along the way, we were taught that it isn't very "Christian" to say no to good people and important causes. After all, if Jesus said yes to the cross, then how can we say no to those comparably painless requests—especially when they could be a blessing to others? For some of us, it's very difficult to say no to worthy requests because we feel like we're not following Jesus when we do so.

Jesus was not a yes-man, though. A quick reading of the Gospels reveals how often He said no. When I first started to notice this theme of Jesus saying no, I didn't know what to do with it. It seemed to cut against the grain of traditional thinking about Jesus. At the end of my study, though, I realized anew that Jesus did not walk the earth as some cosmic bellhop who was at the beck and call of whoever wanted his services. He was intently focused on His Father's will for his life—so much so that anyone else who made a request of Him (outside His Father's will) received a resounding no!

Jesus Said No to Ordinary Human Requests

- When a man in the crowd asked Him to settle an inheritance dispute (an issue that was customarily settled by rabbis), Jesus replied, *No, I wasn't called to be an arbiter between you* (Luke 12:13-14).
- When the people of Capernaum asked Him to continue ministering in their town for a little while longer, Jesus replied, *No, I must preach the good news of the Kingdom of God to the other towns also, because that is why I was sent* (Luke 4:42-43).
- When the healed demoniac asked Him for permission to become one of His disciples, Jesus replied, *No, go home to your family and tell them how much the Lord has done for you* (Mark 5:19).

Jesus Said No to the Crowd's Demands

- When a group of Pharisees and teachers of the law asked Him to perform a miraculous sign, Jesus replied, *No, a wicked and adulterous generation asks for a miraculous sign* (Matt. 12:38-39)!
- When a crowd asked Him to give them the bread He had given them the day before, Jesus replied, *No, I am the bread of life. He who comes to me will never go hungry* (John 6:34-35).

Jesus Said No to Common Sense Requests

- When the disciples asked Him to send away the crowd of five thousand people to could get something to eat, Jesus replied, *No, you give them something to eat* (Luke 9:12-13).
- When a potential follower asked for a little time to bury his father before following Him, Jesus replied, *No, let the spiritually dead bury their own dead* (Matt. 8:21-22).
- When a group of Pharisees asked Him to silence the crowd's shouting as He made His way into Jerusalem, Jesus replied, *No, if they keep quiet, the stones will cry out* (Luke 19:39-40).

Jesus Said No to Close Friends

- When Mary and Martha asked Him to hurry to Bethany so He could heal His close friend Lazarus, Jesus replied, *No,* and He stayed where He was for two more days (John 11:3-6).
- When the mother of two of His closest disciples asked for the right- and left-hand seats next to him in the Kingdom, Jesus replied, *No, you don't know what you are asking* (Matt. 20:21-22).
- When James and John asked Him to call down fire to destroy the Samaritans who had rejected Him, Jesus replied, *No, the Son of Man did not come to destroy men's lives, but to save them* (Luke 9:54-56).
- When Peter asked Him to stop talking about dying on a cross, Jesus replied, *No!* In fact, He said, *Get thee behind me, Satan, no* (Mark 8:32-33)!

- When the disciples asked Him (just before He left them to return to heaven) if He would tell them when the kingdom would be inaugurated, Jesus replied, *No, it is not for you to know the times or dates the Father has set by his own authority* (Acts 1:6-7).[66]

Where in the world did we get the idea that Jesus always said yes? He certainly spent His life serving others, but that didn't mean He always said yes to them. Jesus said no to people and requests whenever it did not line up with the yes He needed to keep saying to the Father.

Three More No's

There was one other significant occasion in which Jesus said no—this time on behalf of another. The story of Mary and Martha (Luke 10:38-42) is frequently heralded as the Scripture that elevates contemplative spirituality over and against social activism. But if this was the point Luke was making, why would he place the parable of the Good Samaritan (10:25-37), a story calling for acts of compassion, immediately before this account? There is a lot more going on here than the pitting of spiritual personality types against each other. Jesus says no to three things that so many of us struggle to say no to:

> As Jesus and his disciples were on their way, he came to a village where a woman named Martha opened her home to him. She had a sister called Mary, who sat at the Lord's feet listening to what he said. But Martha was distracted by all the preparations that had to be made. She came to him and asked, "Lord, don't you care that my sister has left me to do the work by myself? Tell her to help me!"
>
> "Martha, Martha," the Lord answered, "You are worried and upset about many things, but only one thing is needed. Mary has chosen what is better, and it will not be taken away from her."
>
> —Luke 10:38-42

1) Jesus Said No to Lots of Activity

Jesus' no to Martha says a lot about what He was *not* looking for—namely, lots of activity. Luke says Martha was distracted by "all" the preparations that needed to be made. Evidently, she was a busy little bee. But her busy-ness didn't earn her any extra credit with Jesus. He was not necessarily looking for lots of activity. Not only did Jesus refuse to send in Mary to help Martha in the kitchen, He wasn't impressed with the full schedule Martha was trying to keep. In fact, Martha's many activities actually brought a gentle rebuke from Jesus: "You are worried and upset about many things, but only one thing is needed." As Henry Ford said, "A weakness of all human beings is trying to do too many things. That scatters effort and destroys direction. It makes for haste, and haste makes waste."[67]

There is a common reason we say yes to doing so many things: we crave a sense of significance. Our busy schedules become a means of feeling important. In other words, if you want to feel like you are an important part of the church, community, or company, you had better keep doing those things that the organization says are important. Martha undoubtedly saw kingdom-significance in the opportunity to serve Jesus in her home. She naturally jumped at the chance to do something for Him. We probably would have done the same thing. But somewhere along the way, Martha realized she couldn't accomplish the task she had set out to do. Her desire to do something important for Jesus ultimately hit the ceiling of her own limitations.

Hitting the Ceiling of our Limitations

It's actually a gift from God when we hit this ceiling. One of the lies many of us buy into is that God will supply all of the energy, time, and resources we need to give ourselves to any number of good opportunities that come across our paths. We're tempted to believe that because we have an omnipotent God on our side, we are somehow free from the rule of any limitations.

Hitting the ceiling of your limitations should cause you to pause and consider whether what you are doing is really God's will for you, or just something you want to do. There is a difference. If you know that what you are doing is what you are supposed to be doing, then your anxiety about accomplishing that task can give way to the truth that *there is sufficient time to do the whole will of God.* There have been points when I have needed to recite this mantra every hour of the day as a way of reminding myself that God would help me complete the task I was struggling to get done.

There have been other times, though, when my anxiety about accomplishing a task has been the result of my saying yes to someone or something when I should have said no. Perhaps I said yes because of a desire to be part of something important, or because I didn't want to disappoint someone, or because I thought I had enough time to add it to my schedule. Then, when I hit the ceiling of my own limitations, I desperately called on God to bail me out. Oswald Sanders diagnoses the issue for us: "Often the pressure a spiritual leader feels comes from assuming tasks that God has not assigned." Sanders, then, warns us of the consequences for such a course of action: "For such tasks the leader cannot expect God to supply the extra strength required."[68]

Jesus loves to come through for us when we are staying diligently focused on those things He has called us to do. In those cases, we really can rest in the fact that there is sufficient time to do the whole will of God. However, we shouldn't think these words are some magical incantation we can use to manipulate God into bailing us out of commitments He never called us to make. Martha tried to get Jesus to bail her out, too—by asking Him to send Mary into the kitchen to help her. His response to her is instructive. He said no.

Getting Tired for the Right Things

A disclaimer is probably required at this point. The goal in life is not to avoid ever experiencing fatigue. As Sanders continues, "Mediocrity is the result of never getting tired."[69] There is a movement today encouraging Christians to pursue the "balanced life." This objective makes sense in light of how many of us are living without margins or boundaries of any kind. But if the purpose of balance is simply to keep from ever getting tired, then it isn't a big enough goal.

Jesus got tired. It's just that He got tired doing what He knew the Father wanted Him to do. Periodic fatigue will always be the lot for those who spend themselves for God: "On one occasion when Michelangelo was pressing himself to finish a work…someone warned him, 'This may cost your life!' He replied, 'What else is life for?'"[70]

Life is about getting tired for the right things.

The Dangers of Success

The worst thing that can happen to those of us living frantically-paced, disordered lives is we succeed when we take on those things we're not called to do. Nothing keeps us on the treadmill of doing more and more like success. I have felt this the most in the context of ministry success: the youth group outgrew its meeting room, the adult community group I led tripled in size, the people in my church liked and admired me, my public approval rating was high…*and then so was I.*

Success can be intoxicating. Even when it's in a ministry setting, where you're supposed to be serving Jesus, success can blur your thinking about how many things you ought to be doing. I didn't want to let off on the gas for fear of slowing down the rate of ministry success. Even though I could feel myself getting distracted and divided from those specific things I knew God had called me to do, I was tempted to re-double my efforts and act as though my spiritual reserves were sufficient to take on the additional ministry responsibilities. I didn't want to say no, in part, because it would have jeopardized achieving a little more ministry success.

When J. P. Getty, one of the world's first billionaires, was interviewed and asked how much more money he needed, he replied, "Only a little bit more." Just a little bit more is the motto of many people driven to succeed. The taste of success makes you hungry for a little bit more, which in turn keeps you striving a little bit harder. In the end, you find yourself on a treadmill that never lets you off. Why? Because as Robert McGee says, "Today's success never lasts much past midnight. Tomorrow you'll have to do it all over again."[71]

Lily Tomlin once said, "The trouble with being in the rat race is that even if you win, you're still a rat."[72] Fortunately for me, the Spirit of God held up the mirror to what I was doing. Similar to Jesus' rebuke of Martha, He graciously reminded me that He was not looking for lots of activity.

2) Jesus Said No to "Me-Centered Service"

Martha slipped into quite a bit of "me-talk" in her brief conversation with Jesus: "Lord, don't you care that my sister has left *me* to do the work by *myself*? Tell her to help *me*!" (emphasis mine).

Three times in the space of one verse, Martha revealed the self-orientation of her service. It was clear by the words she used, "me," "my," and "me," that Martha's service was more about her than it was about Jesus. She didn't stop to ask Jesus' opinion about the work she was doing. She assumed her agenda was in perfect accord with what Jesus wanted. How could she have known any differently? She didn't even ask Him what He wanted. The closest Martha got to sitting at His feet was when she moved them to dust!

Just because I'm serving in Jesus' name doesn't mean my service can't default to becoming "all about me." It's easy for our eyes to become so focused on our own little kingdom agendas that we fail to take the time to find out if it's even what Jesus wants us to be doing.

Bill had been a Christian for only a few months, when he ran headlong into his first example of me-centered service in the church. It happened on his way into the church kitchen to retrieve some coffee cups for his community group. When Bill stepped across the threshold of the kitchen doorway, he was stopped by the kitchen police.

Helen had been part of the church for a long time. She knew all of the rules and regulations of the kitchen. She had written them. In fact, her spiritual gift seemed to be informing everyone about them. Bill might as well have walked in front of the firing squad. There was no way he was getting out of that kitchen with any coffee cups, not if Helen had anything to say about it. And she did. Helen unloaded both barrels of her kitchen policy manual on him:

- "*I* have created clear procedures for how one obtains kitchen supplies, and you're not following *my* protocol!"
- "*I* have a list with specific people who have authorization to retrieve kitchen supplies, and you're not on *my* list!"

The kitchen had become Helen's little kingdom. As a result, she had lost sight of the One for whom she was supposed to be serving. It was no longer about Jesus and other people. It was about Helen.

Dressing It Up in Spiritual Garb

Most of us who are in charge of things are more socially adept than Helen. Some of us are so good at cloaking me-centered service in spiritual garb that our own personal agendas are never detected. Self-centered service frequently gets overlooked in the life of a church, community, or company. At times, it's because self-centered service actually gets things done.

If you want to play for an Audience of One, though, you need to acknowledge that this kind of service, detected or not, is just an extension of your pride and ego. If productivity was all that Jesus cared about, He would have been content to let Martha keep firing on all cylinders, motivated by her own little kingdom agenda. After all, she was probably getting a lot done. But Jesus loved Martha enough to gently rebuke her and let her know that this was not the kind of service for which He was looking.

A Case Study in Me-Centered Service

Dianne, a mother of three, recently realized her tendency to let me-centered service dictate what she did for the Lord. She tells the story of how she drifted there:

> I knew as clearly as I had known anything in my life that God had called me to adopt and raise children. When the Lord opened a door for my husband and me to bring three children into our home, it was a confirmation of what I knew I was called to do. And in those first few years, I had a resolve and a focus to my life. My priorities were clear. I even calendarized them. I said no to anything and everything that might distract me—in order to stay true to my calling.

> Within a couple of years, though, my focus began to get blurry. At the time, I never would have articulated it that way. I still knew that God had called me to be a mother. It's just that my conviction about raising children became routine, then it became burdensome, and then I started to view it as an obstacle that was keeping me from being able to serve God in "really important" ways.

> It wasn't like I had an affair or abandoned my family. I'm learning that the enemy's tactics are subtler than that. I simply divided my time among so many different serving opportunities (Sunday school

coordinator, Kids Club leader, PTA president, etc.) that the majority of my energy and attention was being spent away from the very ones I knew God had called me to love and serve. The explanation I gave for signing on to so many things was that "these people really needed me." In hindsight, I realize that there was a common denominator to all of my serving: it was my way of getting approval, the kind of affirmation you don't necessarily get from young children.

Things came to a head when I began traveling hundreds of miles several times a year (on my own) in order to spend weeks at a time "caring for" my parents. I told my husband that these trips were about me looking after my parents. How could anyone argue with that? But honestly, there was another motivation lurking behind these visits: I still longed for my parents' approval. Ever since I was a little girl I've felt inferior to my older sister. She had always been the apple of my parents' eye, the one who got their attention and the lion's share of their affections. My hope was that my parents would see the time I was taking to visit them, and begin to look at me the way they longingly looked at my sister. Ironically, none of my efforts to serve my parents ever brought about the desired result. Despite the sacrifices of money, energy, and especially time, the kind of parental approval I wanted so badly never came. I just got more tired. And all the while, my children continued to get the dregs of my time.

Finally, I hit the wall, and woke up to what was happening in my life. God had given me a crystal clear vision for what He wanted me to be doing, and how to be spending my time, and I had let myself become totally sidetracked. It hadn't taken blatant sin to distract me from God's calling on my life—just a craving for approval, mingled with my unwillingness to say no to a lot of "good" opportunities that were out there.

I am resolved again to calendarize what I know God has called me to be about. I'm making the commitment to say no to those serving opportunities that are simply delivery systems for me getting an approval fix so that I can say yes to the Father's will for my life. I'm learning that it takes too much time and energy to try and manage people's opinions of me and stay true to Jesus.

3) Jesus Said No to Ministry

As surprising as it may seem, Jesus' comment to Martha also shows
He was not necessarily looking for ministry. Perhaps you're wondering
if Martha really was doing ministry. Wasn't she just making dinner and
setting the table?

Especially in the first century, hospitality was viewed as a vital form
of ministry. In fact, the clue that Martha was engaged in real ministry is
found in the word Luke uses to describe what she was doing: "Martha
was distracted by all the preparations" (10:40). The Greek word that
stands behind, "preparations," is *diakonia*—from which we get the word
deacon. In other words, Martha was up to her eyeballs in real ministry
responsibilities.

What got Martha so upset was she knew there was someone sitting
in the living room who was more than capable of helping her finish the
diakonia! And yet Martha's request for ministry support was met by
what must have been a shocking response from Jesus: "No, Mary has
chosen what is better, and it will not be taken away from her."

Jesus wanted Martha to know that sitting at His feet was more
important even than doing ministry. This was not his way of elevating
Mary on the basis of her so-called contemplative disposition. "Sitting
at someone's feet" was the phrase used in the first century to describe a
rabbi-disciple relationship. Thus, when Mary sat at Jesus' feet, she was
choosing to be His disciple. Whereas Martha's *words* said Jesus was her
Lord, Mary's *actions* showed He was her Lord. It was Mary's decision
to become a *disciple* that Jesus was referring to when He told Martha
that her sister had "chosen what is better."

Don't be too hard on Martha. In her day, women weren't supposed
to sit at a rabbi's feet. That was way outside the religious box. There
were certain roles that were culturally acceptable for women, and certain
roles that were absolutely taboo. Practicing hospitality was acceptable.
Becoming the disciple of a respected rabbi was not. Jesus took the lid
off the box, though, and invited women to sit at His feet, too. And
despite what everyone (including Martha) would have thought about
her, Mary decided to take Jesus up on His invitation. Talk about playing
for an Audience of One!

Not only did Mary cut against the grain of cultural and religious expectations, she was also willing to appear lazy, sitting at the feet of Jesus while Martha was slaving away in the kitchen. For most of us, appearing to be lazy is like committing 'reputation suicide.' That's part of what motivates us to spin the description of our schedules. We want to appear busier than we really are. On the other hand, some of us are so concerned about avoiding even the appearance of spiritual laziness that we actually try and fill every moment of our lives with ministry activities. Then we wear our ministry calendar around like either a badge of justification or a mark of martyrdom.

The Biggest "Ministry Badge" Culprits

Unfortunately, it's often those who are supposed to be spiritually mature who are most guilty of wearing ministry activity badges. For example, when it came time for Pastor Richard to share the highlights of his summer with a small group of ministry colleagues, he made certain to lead off with the part of his report he wanted his peers to remember: "Well, I only had one day off all summer." Whatever else he was going to share with his fellow pastors about his summer, he wanted to make sure they viewed it through the lens of an incredible work ethic and a schedule chock full of ministry tasks.

Why do we do that? Are we so scared of looking lazy that we paint a self-portrait that exaggerates our busy features? Here is the irony of the matter: busy-ness isn't the opposite of laziness. Busy-ness is a form of laziness. Busy-ness is being too lazy to intentionally and prayerfully say no so we can sit at Jesus' feet, listen for His still small voice, and then be obedient to do only those things He calls us to do—regardless of whether or not it makes us appear lazier than our peers.

Martha could have been setting the table, preaching a sermon, or doing a miracle of healing. It wouldn't have mattered. Jesus would have responded the same way, regardless of what ministry task she was engaged in. He wanted Martha to know nothing was as important as sitting at His feet. Not because sitting at His feet was necessarily *opposed* to her ministry, but because sitting at His feet would *inform* her ministry. Jesus wanted Martha to know that the only way using her gift of hospitality would have meaning and significance in the kingdom was if it flowed out of "sitting at His feet."

A Case Study in Saying No to Ministry

Steve was gifted and called to do pastoral ministry. He was also champing at the bit to get into the game by the time he graduated with his ministry degree. However, during his engagement to his fiancée, Heather, he confided in me what he believed God was calling him *not* to do. While sitting at Jesus' feet one day and reflecting on the words of Deuteronomy 24:5, he sensed he was supposed to say no to pastoral ministry for the first year of their marriage in order to better say yes to the next assignment God had in mind for him:

> If a man has recently married, he must not be sent to war or have any other duty laid on him. For one year he is to be free to stay at home and bring happiness to the wife he has married.
>
> —Deut. 24:5

Jesus was calling Steve to love, bless, and serve his wife during the first year of their marriage. But with that calling to do something came an equally important calling to say no to doing something good. Steve knew Jesus had spoken to him. And at first he heeded the assignment with contentment. But then a wonderful youth ministry opportunity came knocking on his door. It was a chance for Steve to do what he knew God had gifted him to do. It was an opportunity to do something he knew would have a kingdom impact. Steve began to contemplate how saying yes to this ministry invitation would be a good thing: the position was only half time, he could still learn how to love, serve and bless his wife, and perhaps a part-time ministry position would actually be a helpful transition for the years of full-time ministry that lay ahead of them. After all, he reasoned, the ministry opportunity had come knocking on his door. It wasn't like he had gone looking for it.

But not every open door is a door opened by God.

Though tempted to renege on his vow, in the end, Steve stayed true to the word Jesus had impressed upon him. God's voice was louder in his ears than the luring voice of a significant ministry opportunity. He said no to a fantastic ministry invitation in order to say yes to the simple task Jesus had given him for his first year of marriage. Steve undoubtedly would have done some great things had he taken that ministry position, but it wouldn't have been God's best for his life.

Jesus honored Steve's faithfulness to say no, too. During their first year of marriage, God united Steve and Heather around a lifelong vision for serving the church and the world. And in the years since saying that difficult no, they have been led into ministry ventures where they have made a real kingdom impact. Even more importantly than that, though, they are experiencing God's approval along the way.

Choosing the "Best" over the "Good"

The enemy of God's best is rarely that which is evil, but that which is good. That's what makes saying no (even to good things) so important. If we don't learn to say no, we'll probably end up doing a lot of good things, but we'll fall short of the best God intends for us.

The fact that Mary sat down at Jesus' feet meant she was willing to say no to a lot of things. She was willing to say no to playing the culturally expected role of a woman in the first century. She was willing to say no to her sister's indignant request to help her—even though she probably appeared lazy in the process. She was even willing to say no to an important ministry opportunity. It is no wonder Jesus was so proud of Mary. The voice of her neighbors (and her sister) was not ruling her schedule anymore. Mary was sitting at Jesus' feet, and becoming more attuned to what He wanted her to be doing with her life. In turn, her courage to play for an Audience of One was rewarded with His word of approval: "Mary has chosen what is better...."

It's not that disciples just sit at Jesus' feet and soak up spiritual knowledge all day. Mary sat at the Lord's feet and listened for His voice *so that* she could find out what He wanted her to do...and then do it. We are called to do something, too. Jesus is not taking issue with ministry per se, or opposing our efforts to do things for Him. The point of the story is that Mary, unlike Martha, understood the order of *first* sitting at Jesus' feet and listening for His voice, and *then* doing what He called her to do.

It's at Jesus' feet where we discover our calling; it's also at His feet where we learn what we are not called to be doing.

Admittedly, it is a struggle to say yes to God's best and no to the rest. The only way to keep them straight is to take time to sit at Jesus' feet and listen for His voice. But if you don't settle the issue of being willing to say no, it won't matter what He calls you to do when you hear His voice. Satan will distract you from God's best with invitations from good people and all manner of worthwhile causes.

One final word of warning: when you say no, you need to be prepared for any number of negative responses. People may be disappointed or frustrated with you. They may think you're lazy. They may think you're backsliding in your faith. They may question your commitment to the cause. That's why saying no to ministry opportunities may be the most difficult no of all for you to say. It also might be the most crucial step to take in learning to play for an Audience of One. Stop feeling guilty when you say no. You're in good company when you do so. After all, even Jesus said no!

Prayer for Eternal Perspective on our Time

"Teach us to number our days aright that we might gain a heart of wisdom."

—Moses (Psalm 90:12)

Going Deeper

1. Prayerfully do an inventory with your schedule. Are there things that have found their way onto your calendar because you didn't say no when you needed to? Get specific.

2. In those moments when you begin to feel yourself getting anxious about whether you will be able to complete something you really sense God has called you to do, reflect on and then recite, "There is sufficient time to do the whole will of God."

3. Who and what are the people, activities, and events you have the most difficulty saying no to? Name them. Ask yourself why it's so difficult to say no to them. Are you concerned about their opinion of you? Are you afraid to appear lazy to them? Surrender this aspect of your reputation to God.

4. Finish out your commitment to those people to whom you should have said no. Playing for an Audience of One does not justify breaking your word. But then pray for the courage and resolve to say no when your commitment is up and you are asked again.

5. Practice responding to invitations, requests, or ministry opportunities with the words, "Let me pray about that," as a way of not saying yes in the heat of the moment. Then go home and actually sit at Jesus' feet, and listen to see if He has an opinion about it.

6. Be proactive about periodically sitting at Jesus' feet, specifically asking Him to order your days, and give you direction about what He wants you to be doing.

Chapter 8

Transferring the Title

*"I have held many things in my hands and I have lost them all.
But whatever I have placed in God's hands that I still possess."*
—Martin Luther

I GREW UP in the 1980's, during the heyday of television evangelists. As a teenager, I tuned in to a couple of prosperity gospel preachers in particular. Not because I was especially interested in spiritual matters, but because I got a real kick out of listening to them make their slick sales pitches. I was fairly ignorant about God at the time, but I still knew there was something fishy about these preachers' messages, which sounded the same each week and always concluded with the application step: *send me your money and God will make you rich!*

I remember when a couple of those televangelists were unveiled as frauds and sent to jail. The fallout from the scandals was devastating to the church's reputation. It left a blemish on the face of Christianity for the whole world to see. Skeptics confidently dismissed any form of organized religion because they assumed there was a straight-line continuum between what was being depicted on the nightly news and what was happening at every local church. For many people, the televangelist debacle reinforced in their minds that Christianity was a religion for suckers, a moneymaking operation that preyed on the naïve.

Not only were the televangelist scandals destructive to the church's ability to effectively reach out, they also shattered the trust of many within the church. Believers became a little less inclined to give pastors the benefit of the doubt, especially when it was money they were talking about from the pulpit.

When I recommitted my life to Jesus, I started attending a church. The pastor had an outstanding reputation in the community. There never had been a hint of financial impropriety in the church's history. And yet on those occasions when the pastor would teach about money, I immediately became wary. Almost involuntarily, I could sense my defenses going up. I would steel myself for some version of the prosperity gospel application step that I had heard so many times on television. It never came. There was nothing unbiblical in what that pastor taught with regard to money. The problem was with me. I was paranoid by the memories of television preachers who had misused their position for financial gain.

I wasn't the only one in America who was skeptical of preachers talking about money. James Patterson and Peter Kim, authors of *The Day America Told the Truth*, took the pulse of the nation on this matter, and here's what they discovered:

> When a national survey asked respondents to rank various professions for their honesty and integrity, TV evangelists came out almost at the very bottom, below lawyers, politicians, car salesman, and even prostitutes. Out of the seventy-three occupations compared in this integrity rating, only two ended up lower on the scale: organized crime bosses and drug dealers![73]

In order to distance myself from the TV evangelist reputation, I resolved never to talk about money in the same breath I talked about God. My motive for keeping them separate was simple: I didn't want people to think I was a religious gold-digger. More importantly, I didn't want the gospel I was sharing to resemble in any way the prosperity gospel they might have seen on television. I thought the best way to protect the gospel from "guilt by association" was to steer completely clear of the money topic. One of my mantras during those days was: "I don't want to talk about money; I just want to share the gospel!" I would say this with a chip on my shoulder, feeling spiritually superior for avoiding the potentially sensitive and offensive topic of money.

The Great Divide Between Faith and Finances

Many American Christians have similar feelings about keeping matters of faith and finances separate. Robert Wuthnow, in his book, *God and Mammon in America*, writes:

> There appears to be a major disconnection between the people's religious beliefs and how they use money. If a single word had to be used to describe the relationship between religion and money, it would be *compartmentalization*.[74]

Research continues to show there is little connection between most American Christians' faith and the way we view and use our money. Today, the typical American family is twice as wealthy as it was forty years ago—even after factoring in cost of living increases and inflation. Yet giving has declined almost every year since 1968. In fact, as John and Sylvia Ronsvalle highlight, at the depth of the Great Depression (1933), the average giving percentage of a typical church member was 3.3 percent. By 2000, after a half century of unprecedented prosperity, church members only gave an average of 2.6 percent of their incomes—about one fourth of a tithe.[75]

Money is not just a stumbling block for those *outside* the church. It is a struggle for many who are *inside* it as well.

If we are going to get serious about playing for an Audience of One, we eventually must broach the topic of finances. Despite the fact that some religious leaders have misused their platforms for money, we need to let the truth of the gospel inform what we do with our finances. The soul of Christianity is shriveling today, in part, because while the idol of Mammon continues to gain followers, local churches, in the name of seeker sensitivity, remain silent about how to please God with our money. Some of us have been content to keep our faith and our finances separate for so long that it seems normal to us. But it is this compartmentalized way of thinking that Martin Luther was confronting when he said:

If you preach the gospel in all aspects with the exception of the issues, which deal specifically with your day and age, you are not preaching the gospel at all.[76]

Bridging the Great Divide

So what happened in Jesus' day and age when the truth of the gospel met the issue of money? The story of Levi, the tax collector, gives us a glimpse.

Jesus went out and saw a tax collector by the name of Levi sitting at his tax booth. "Follow me," Jesus said to him, and Levi got up, left everything and followed him.

—Luke 5:27-28

First, a little bit of historical context: In the first century, tax collectors were not typically candidates for becoming disciples of well-respected rabbis. By and large, they were a despised lot. Jewish tax collectors, like Levi, were especially hated by their fellow countrymen. They were viewed as sell-outs to the Roman government—sort of a Benedict Arnold and an IRS agent all rolled into one.

Rome used tax collectors to do the dirty work of gathering tax revenue from all the people living within the boundaries of their empire. Basically, they would subcontract out the job to whoever made the highest bid. The tax collector's bid was based on what he thought he could extract from the people. Then whatever money he could squeeze out of the people, over and above his bid to Rome, became his income. So the way most tax collectors made a living (and then some) was by burdening the people with a much heavier tax load than they were actually required by Rome to pay.

You can imagine why the Pharisees were so upset when they discovered Jesus cavorting with Levi and his motley crew of tax collectors. According to them, nobody worth their spiritual salt would have had anything to do with this kind of people. To even associate with a tax collector was considered by the first century religious leaders as morally reprehensible.

We don't know the details of why Levi initially took the job. Maybe he desperately needed money for his family. Maybe he never bothered to learn a trade. Perhaps it was just good, old-fashioned greed that motivated him. But one thing is for sure: when Levi decided to become a tax collector, he was knowingly exchanging his spiritual life and the fellowship of his faith community for money. Once he made that decision, he knew he would live with those consequences for the rest of his life. He knew he would be forever marked as an "outcast" by the religious leadership.

Levi became rich, but at what price? Was it worth it? Did his ability to buy more stuff really fill the spiritual void in his life? Is it even possible to make enough money to buy happiness? Donald Trump, the billionaire real estate tycoon, thinks so. He once said, "Whoever says money can't buy happiness doesn't know where to shop."[77]

Of course, Trump is the minority voice among those with great wealth. John W. Rockefeller confessed, "I have made millions, but they have brought me no happiness." W. H. Vanderbilt once said, "The care of two hundred million dollars is enough to kill anyone. There is no pleasure in it." Andrew Carnegie gave commentary on the relationship between riches and happiness when he noted, "Millionaires seldom smile."[78]

There's nothing inherently wrong with having money. Money can purchase many good things. It's just that it can't buy lasting fulfillment. One author wrote about what money can and cannot buy:

A bed but not sleep;
Books but not brains;
Food but not appetite;
Finery but not beauty;
A house but not a home;
Medicine but not health;
Luxuries but not culture;
Amusements but not happiness;
Religion but not salvation;
A passport to everywhere but heaven.[79]

Unless Levi had a very high tolerance for loneliness and rejection, it probably didn't take long for him to regret his decision to become a tax collector. Unfortunately, there are some holes out of which we can't dig ourselves. Levi was in one of those pits. It wasn't as simple as resigning from his tax collector's post and getting another job. He couldn't just go out and choose a different vocation. He would have been blackballed from working with any reputable business. His name was as good as mud with the Jewish community. Nobody would have associated with a "sinner" like Levi—even if he were to quit his job. Once a tax collector, always a tax collector.

Then one day Jesus saw Levi sitting at his tax collector's booth, and He spoke the most amazing grace-filled invitation to Levi that he had ever heard in his life: "Follow Me." Imagine what Levi must have thought when he heard those two little words. There was no way he could have anticipated this invitation. Levi probably wondered to himself, *How could someone like Jesus, a respected rabbi, invite someone like me, into his intimate circle of followers?*

This was nothing less than an opportunity to be back in relationship with God. No wonder Levi got up, left everything, and followed Jesus. He instinctively knew that compartmentalizing his faith from his finances would have been an unacceptable response to such a lavish expression of grace. "Leaving everything" wasn't especially virtuous on Levi's part. It was the only appropriate response to Jesus' invitation.

Levi wasn't the first disciple to "leave everything." Peter, James, and John did the same thing when Jesus called them to follow Him. After Jesus amazed these fishermen with a miraculous catch, He gave them a vision for what they could be doing with their lives. He offered them the vocational opportunity of a lifetime, and in response to that invitation, Luke says:

> They pulled their boats up on shore, left everything, and followed him.
>
> —Luke 5:11

It's as though people knew the only appropriate response to Jesus' invitation to follow Him was to "leave everything." There was no compartmentalizing of one's faith and finances. They went hand in hand. It reminds me of what Sam Houston, the famous war hero and politician, did after he decided to follow Christ. According to Randy Alcorn:

> After his baptism, Houston said he wanted to pay half the local minister's salary. When someone asked him why, he responded, "My pocketbook was baptized, too."[80]

When Levi began following Jesus, his pocketbook got baptized, too.

"Vow of Poverty" vs. "Throwing a Party"

It might sound surprising, but the application step to this story is not that you need to get rid of all your belongings and take a vow of poverty. It's understandable how a quick reading of Levi's response might lead one to that conclusion. After all, Scripture does say he left everything and followed Jesus. But there is more going on here than first meets the eye. It's critical to notice what Levi did *after* he left everything:

> Then Levi held a great banquet.
>
> —Luke 5:29

In the first century, banquets were feasts—not a church potluck where those at the end of the line are left to decide between the last scoop of green bean casserole and tapioca surprise. Banquets were costly events for the host. In fact, the size and quality of the banquet was one of the ways society measured the social standing of the host. Banquets were status symbols, sort of like how some people today measure status by the kind of car you drive: a Rolls Royce on one end of the spectrum and, say, a Yugo on the other end. (Of course, even owning a Yugo today makes one wealthy in comparison to much of the world's population!) In the same way, even the ability to host a banquet in the first century was an indication of significant financial means. And Luke specifies the kind of banquet Levi hosted: a "great banquet."

This word *great* was not simply Luke's way of giving commentary on the food's quality, but his way of describing the banquet's size. The Greek that stands behind *great* is *mega*—as in megaphone or mega-church. This little prefix dramatically affects the meaning of the word it precedes. The point Luke is making is this: Levi didn't throw an ordinary, average-sized banquet, or even a really large banquet. He threw a mega-banquet. It was a Rolls Royce banquet!

This should cause us to pause and ask: *How could Levi still afford to throw a banquet at all, much less a mega-banquet? He had just left everything. How can we reconcile "Levi left everything" with "Then Levi held a mega-banquet?"*

It only makes sense when we understand the significance of the two little words that clarify the One for whom Levi was throwing this banquet. Luke is very precise at this point:

> Then Levi held a great banquet *for Jesus.*
>
> —Luke 5:29, emphasis mine

When Levi left everything to follow Jesus, it didn't mean he was taking a vow of poverty. "Leaving everything" was Luke's shorthand way of saying Levi was "transferring the title of all his money and possessions into Jesus' name." Levi's money would no longer be used "for Levi." It would be used "for Jesus." And his first act of living out the implications of this title transfer was to throw a great banquet for Jesus.

Keeping Up With the Joneses

Unlike the banquets Levi certainly had thrown in the past, this one wasn't about showing off his wealth, or trying to impress his fellow tax collectors. His money was no longer being used to portray a certain image to his peers. He wasn't playing for their approval or applause anymore. He was playing for an Audience of One with his money.

Some people play the game of trying to keep up with the Joneses. Who are the Joneses anyway? Basically they're anyone whose opinions move us to spend money on things we wouldn't otherwise purchase in order to manage the way we look in their eyes. It could be family members, friends, co-workers, neighbors, or even strangers. Most of us don't like to play this game, but at times, we find ourselves doing it anyway. Some of us spend money on all sorts of things to impress other people. It could be the clothes we wear, the cars we drive, the home we live in, or the presents we give.

Others of us aren't as driven to spend money trying to impress the Joneses as we are prone to spend money in ways that allow us to at least look respectable in their eyes. We don't want to feel like we're living several rungs below them on the social ladder. But using money to show off or to avoid shame are two sides of the same coin. Both motivations are evidence that our ears are more attuned to our neighbors' voices than to the One whose voice we ought to be listening to.

The Other "Audience of one"

It's not just our neighbors' voices that drive what we do with our money, though. It's also the gnawing sound of our own appetite. Studies reveal that there has been a steady increase in spending on luxury items in the United States. In 1950, 10 percent of our income was spent on some form of self-indulgence. By 1980, spending on the same kind of luxury items went up to 30 percent of our income.[81] That trend is continuing. Many of us are playing for a different audience of one (ourselves!) when it comes to how we use our money.

That's what makes Levi's response so countercultural. When he threw a great banquet for Jesus, he was demonstrating that he was no longer using his money to impress his neighbors or indulge his own appetite. Levi's first financial move with his newly redeemed money had a completely different purpose. It served to advance Jesus' agenda in his sphere of influence. Luke tells us what happened as a result of Levi's great banquet: *a large crowd of tax collectors came to the party and met Jesus.*

Money's Ministry Potential

Once Levi transferred the title of all he owned into Jesus' name, his money became anointed with kingdom possibility. He was able to finance a great banquet, and in so doing, he got a lot of his spiritually needy friends into the same room with Jesus. There may have been no more effective way for Levi to reach his fellow tax collectors than to host this banquet. But hosting a banquet costs money. Bill Hybels, the pastor of Willow Creek Community Church, tells the story of how theologian R.C. Sproul once asked him how much ministry he could do with a hundred dollars:

> I assumed he was hoping for some deep theological response, but before I could think of one he answered the question himself: "You can do about a hundred dollars' worth." He was simply making the point that a fruitful ministry requires resources.[82]

It takes money to do ministry.

That's why Jesus isn't necessarily looking for His followers to get rid of all their money and take a vow of poverty. In some ways, taking a vow of poverty might be simpler than transferring the title of all our possessions into Jesus' name and staying on to manage the funds. The dangers of money are real. The warnings in Scripture are clear. If we take a vow of poverty, we'll protect ourselves from the temptations of wealth. If we take a vow of poverty, we'll never have to risk that some day we might stop surrendering our money to God. But since when is God's highest priority the elimination of the possibility of sin? The risk that we may hoard or indulge is worth it to God. He would rather give us the opportunity to steward His resources—even given the possibility that we could be selfish with it—than strip us of the freedom to keep choosing to throw great banquets for Jesus. God is pleased when we continually lay ourselves, and our money on the altar.

The antidote to the perils of money is not to blindly get rid of it, but to transfer the title of all you have into Jesus' name, and then look for ways to invest that money for His kingdom purposes. Not only is God honored every time you choose to invest your financial resources this way, but you, too, will experience the incredible joy that comes from knowing something as ordinary as your money is changing the landscape of heaven. Money truly has the potential to impact eternity:

> As base a thing as money is, it yet can be transmuted into everlasting treasure. It can be converted into food for the hungry and clothing for the poor; it can keep a missionary actively winning lost men to the

light of the gospel and thus transmute itself into heavenly values. Any temporal possession can be turned into everlasting wealth. Whatever is given to Christ is immediately touched with immortality.[83]

That's what happened to Levi's money. When he transferred the title of all his money and possessions into Jesus' name, it was immediately touched with immortality. It became anointed to advance God's Kingdom in his sphere of influence. The same thing can happen with our money, too, when it's given over to Jesus. Just think about what God could do through you if you stopped compartmentalizing your faith and finances. How might your "banquets thrown for Jesus" impact eternity?

Harold and Esther were just two ordinary, blue-collar workers whose love for the Lord inspired them to do something with their money that would keep impacting eternity long after they went to heaven. Their vision was to support overseas missionaries for generations to come. That dream moved them to commit a portion of their income each month (above their regular giving) to a secret fund that was revealed at Harold's memorial service. Although Harold and Esther never held high paying jobs, their simple lifestyle and their commitment to let their money serve eternal purposes culminated in a million-dollar endowment. The interest from that fund is being used to support overseas missionary work from now until Jesus returns!

The "So That" Behind God's Blessing

What makes the prosperity gospel I saw on television so dangerous is there is a grain of truth mingled in with the lie. After all, there are times when God does prosper His people with material blessings; when He does open up the floodgates of heaven and pour out so much blessing upon us we cannot contain it (Mal. 3:10). The lie is that *personal* prosperity is God's ultimate goal for His people. It's not. Prosperity is always a means to a far more important end. Throughout the Scriptures there is always a "so that" attached whenever God chooses, blesses, or anoints:

- God chose Abraham *so that* all nations would be blessed through him (Gen. 12:3).

- God blessed Israel *so that* they might be a light to the Gentiles (Isa. 49:6).
- God anointed Jesus *so that* all who call on him might be saved (Romans 10:13).

In a similar way, God pours out His material blessings upon some people so that they might use those resources to bless the rest of the world. Have you ever wondered why you have so much while there are others around the world living in absolute poverty? Here's what the apostle Paul wrote to a group of Christians in Corinth about God's purpose behind their financial surplus:

> You will be made rich in every way *so that* you can be generous on every occasion.
>
> —2 Cor. 9:11, emphasis mine

Like the vast majority of Western Christians, the Corinthian believers had more money than they needed. What they lacked was God's perspective regarding their extra. They were in danger of buying into the first century's version of the prosperity gospel, which promoted the idea (and still does) that an individual's surplus is the end goal of God's blessing. Paul was trying to help the Corinthians grasp the truth that God intends our surplus to be a means of blessing others. As Randy Alcorn wrote in *The Treasure Principle*, "God prospers me not to raise my standard of living, but to raise my standard of giving."[84]

John Wesley, who spearheaded the Methodist revival in England in the eighteenth century, lived out this treasure principle. In his first year in the pastorate, Wesley made thirty pounds. His needs required that he live on twenty-eight pounds, so he gave away the remaining two pounds. In his second year, he made sixty pounds. He lived on twenty-eight pounds and gave away the remaining thirty-two. In his fourth year, he made one hundred twenty pounds. He lived on twenty-eight pounds, and gave away the remaining ninety-two. You see a pattern? God prospered him not to raise his standard of *living*, but to raise his standard of *giving*. (I've joked with our church board about the other pattern within this story: that the doubling of Pastor Wesley's salary should be the model for our salary increases!)

The Joy of Giving

Even if I were to get that kind of raise, though, it wouldn't be so that our family could drive a fancier car, buy new wardrobes, or increase our entertainment budget. Frankly, we would just love the opportunity to throw more banquets for Jesus. I hesitate in writing that for fear of sounding self-righteous. But I desperately want to communicate the deep joy you can experience when you transfer the title of all your money and possessions into Jesus' name. In a day and age when 80 percent of divorcing couples cite financial conflict as a major contributor to their marital problems, I thank God that "money" has been one of the most satisfying aspects of my marriage. You read that last sentence correctly.

It really has been an incredible privilege for Amanda and I to let our temporal possessions become transmuted into everlasting treasures. Money's place in our relationship didn't start out that way, though. Like most couples, we had our battles over money, particularly in our early days together. But there was a crisis point when our attitude and perspective on money changed: *the day we transferred the title of what little money and possessions we had into Jesus' name.*

I'll never forget that day. We were recently engaged, and for months we had been struggling to work through some financial decisions. Unfortunately, we just kept coming to an impasse about how to proceed. One of my favorite marriage sayings is, "When you get married, you become one…and then you spend the rest of your marriage battling over which one of you you'll become!" That's what was happening between us whenever we needed to make a decision about money. We kept battling with one another about who was going to get their way.

Finally, frustration morphed into desperation. We were so tired of how our finances had become a sticking point in our relationship that in the middle of our argument (I mean "discussion"), we literally got down on our knees, held hands, and verbally surrendered our money to God. We actually said out loud, "It's all Yours, Lord. What little we have, and whatever You give us in the future—it's Yours. Now, please help us."

We knew intellectually God was the Owner of everything we had, but previous to that moment we had never articulated it to Him in a prayer of surrender. To be honest, it wasn't a real sentimental moment for either of us. We actually went to prayer in spite of our feelings. After all, praying with someone when you're angry isn't exactly the natural response. But today, with the vantage point of over a decade of marriage behind us, Amanda and I both look back on that moment when we transferred the title of all we had into Jesus' name as the day when we were set free with our money. It was the watershed moment in our stewardship journey, the point when we opened up ourselves to the possibility of true joy in the area of our finances.

Passing the Stewardship Baton

Nearly as exciting as our own journey has been the opportunity we've had to invite others into a stewardship adventure. Last year, I sensed the Lord calling me to do a four-month teaching series on the stewardship of money with our entire church family. I realize there is a fine line between courage and stupidity. Some said that in preaching on money for *four months,* I was flirting with that line. To be honest, I had some apprehension about doing it, too, but I knew it was what God was calling me to do.

The deep work God did in the hearts of His people during that stewardship series was amazing. Seeing so many become joyful, obedient givers was one of the most rewarding experiences of my ministry. People not only got their financial ducks in a row, but in some cases, even marriages were transformed as a result. Doug and Shannon sent me a letter a few months after we wrapped up the stewardship series, describing their journey. Here's a portion of what they shared with me:

In the past, finances and budgeting (or the lack thereof) has been a major struggle for Doug and me. We grew up in very different homes: Doug in a modest Christian home and me in a lavish non-Christian home. As we tried to face our finances, our foundations were so different that it caused major friction. For me, I felt like I was being controlled and judged. For Doug, he felt a tremendous sense of stress at providing for us. So we just avoided the topic.

Last year as we began to study what God's Word says about our money, we had no idea what an amazing journey the Lord wanted to take us on. At the halfway point in the series, we committed to doing a budget. We actually sat down and ruthlessly wrote it out. I was very wary of doing this because it had been such a major source of stress in the past. But the day we created our budget was absolutely transforming to our marriage. We tackled a budget for the first time as a team with the knowledge that God had a plan for our money. We actually walked away from the budget exercise excited about what God could do through our finances.

Little did we know…the process has been, and continues to be so much bigger than just a budget. I've realized that I grew up believing in the "I deserve" ideology. When deciding on a purchase I looked for the very best we could afford and then made my decision based on that—whether it was clothing, a home, or anything in between. I remember the Sunday you talked about living with a wartime strategy. I was pretty uncomfortable. You were definitely pushing some of my buttons! But in praying over the past few months I'm realizing that my filter for making choices was created by the world and not by the Lord. I've begun praying, "Lord, what is the best choice?" All of a sudden that latte on a day when the kids are grumpy and I'm stressing out is not the best answer. Instead, I've found myself asking the Lord to step into my stress. And you know what? He's way better than a sugar-free vanilla latte!

After our first month of what we thought would be a really tight budget we found out that we were a little bit ahead. With the extra we were actually able to pray and divvy that money up for different things that the Lord laid on our hearts. Talk about addicting! When looking back at the things we've "given up" I've realized that I don't even miss them. Besides, some vital ministries have gotten a little bit more leverage to be the hands and feet of Jesus as a result.

We're also in the process of moving from our 3,000 square foot home to a simple 1,200 square foot home. The house costs less than one third of the home we're in now. My non-Christian family thinks we're nuts, but we feel like we're on the ride of a lifetime. As we step closer to the Lord and find out more about what is important to Him instead of what we "deserve," Christ is stripping the unimportant things of life from us. As this happens, our vision is becoming clear and we are able to see, hear, and experience Him the way He intended. This is only the beginning of what I sense the Lord is leading us into!

Just as exciting as watching adults catch a vision for what God can do with money, though, has been passing the stewardship baton on to youth and children. Upon first arriving in Warm Beach, Amanda and I became aware of a single mother who was trying to raise three children without any consistent form of transportation. She had a full-time job, but her paycheck simply didn't stretch far enough to pay the rent, buy the groceries, and purchase a used car. As we prayed for this family, Amanda felt nudged to invite her junior high girls' small group to join her in asking God to provide this family with an automobile. In a sense, the vision to include Amanda's small group in this adventure would "kill two birds with one stone":

1. It would help a family in our church get a car.
2. It would be an object lesson to some junior high girls about the joy of giving.

When Amanda first shared the idea with the girls, a couple of them looked at her with blank stares. After all, they were just kids. They didn't have real jobs. But as Amanda told them real-life stories of God's provision from our lives, the girls' faith grew. They began to dream about God giving them similar stories. The junior high girls decided they would earmark any additional or unexpected monies that came their way for this automobile project. Then they began to pray specifically for God to make them rich so that they could buy this family a car.

Be careful what you pray for ...

Ridiculously lucrative babysitting opportunities opened up that very week. Each Wednesday night, the girls would report back to their small group about how God had given them moneymaking ventures that they weren't even expecting. Special gifts seemed to come out of nowhere. This pattern continued week in and week out. Each experience of God's financial blessing catalyzed them to pray for more money, always with a "so that" attached: "Make us rich, Lord, *so that* we can buy this family a car!"

Over the course of just a few months, these junior high girls watched God answer this prayer. And when they sensed they had enough money to purchase a dependable car, they began to pray for God to provide just the right one. Days later, an elderly gentleman from the community drove into the church parking lot looking for someone who might like to buy his car. He explained he was too old to drive anymore, and he felt led to give someone in our church the opportunity to buy his car at a significantly discounted price. The girls had more than enough to purchase it. Their vision had become a reality!

The junior high girls decided to give the car to the family anonymously. They weren't looking for any thanks, rewards, or applause. The joy they experienced in giving was thanks enough. The thrill of participating with God to buy a car for a family was their reward. The smile they could sense on God's face was their applause!

A Word About Tithing

Exploring the theme of playing for an Audience of One with money would be incomplete without at least referencing the concept of tithing. Although the Old Testament is full of references to tithing, there are only three New Testament scriptures where tithing is specifically mentioned. All three of them are in the context of Jesus taking on the Pharisees for the way they practiced their legalistic spirituality (Matt. 23:23; Luke 11:42, 18:12). Here is a sample of what He said to the Pharisees about their tithing:

> Woe to you, teachers of the law and Pharisees, you hypocrites! You give a tenth of your spices—mint, dill, and cumin. But you have neglected the more important matters of the law—justice, mercy, and faithfulness. You should have practiced the latter, without neglecting the former.
>
> —Matt. 23:23

There's a lot of debate about whether tithing is still to be practiced today by followers of Jesus. Some Christians advocate that tithing has been, and will always be, what Scripture calls for. Others argue that Jesus revoked the Old Testament tithing laws and freed us simply to give when we feel so moved. So which is it?

Based on His teaching in Matthew 23, we can boil down what Jesus says about tithing to three main points:

1. Tithing is not to be a badge of justification.
2. Tithing is not to be the end goal of giving.
3. Tithing is not to be "neglected"

Jesus rebuked the Pharisees for their legalistic practice of tithing, but it was really their *legalism* with which he took issue—not their *tithing*. Jesus was challenging the kind of giving that is done as a means of trying to justify oneself before God. He was making it known that giving 10 percent is not *the* mark of spiritual maturity. That said, Jesus was just as clear in saying the practice of tithing was not to be "neglected" (Matt. 23:23) or "left undone" (Luke 11:42). This is significant because it shows Jesus never rescinded the Old Testament law regarding tithing. He called for a "both/and" view of giving. He wanted His disciples to tithe *and* attend to the more important matters of the law: justice, mercy, and faithfulness.

Summarizing Jesus' teaching: He endorsed the practice of tithing. He upheld it as still being authoritative for His followers. Basically, He said there is nothing wrong with tithing, so long as it doesn't become a badge of pride or the end goal of giving. In other words, tithing is a great *starting* point for giving, but it's not *the* point.

Three Ways of Approaching the Tithe

1. When the tithe becomes religious compartmentalization ...

Some believe the lie that as long as you give 10 percent of your income to God, then you get to use the other 90 percent however you want. But the idea that God is only interested in 10 percent of our money is just another form of religious compartmentalization. In fact, even in the Old Testament, giving God the first 10 percent was meant to serve as a reminder to Israel that the other 90 percent belonged to Him as well. Tithing was never the end goal. That's why God also called His people to take care of the poor who were in their midst (Deut. 15). Making sure the poor were cared for couldn't be broken down into a nice, neat giving percentage. It called Israel to attend to the more important matters of the Law. It called them to a full surrender of their possessions to God.

That's exactly what happened in the earliest days of the church:

> There were no needy persons among them. For from time to time those who owned lands or houses sold them, brought the money from the sales and put it at the apostles' feet, and it was distributed to anyone as he had need.
>
> —Acts 4:34-35

The reason Jesus condemned the Pharisees' religion of the 10 percent is because God wants it all. As W. Graham Scroggie pointed out, "There are two ways in which a Christian may view his money: How much of my money shall I use for God or how much of God's money shall I use for myself?"[85]

2. When "grace" becomes a license for giving less than a tithe ...

Other Christians argue that because Jesus inaugurated an age of grace, we're no longer required to tithe. The idea is that "grace" motivates better than "law." I agree. Biblical grace will move us beyond what the law could do. Unfortunately, the research shows that many well-meaning believers' actual giving (supposedly inspired by grace) is less than the Old Testament's minimum standard of obedience. The average giving percentage of American Christians is about 2.5 percent. It seems pretty tragic that New Testament grace is only one fourth as effective as the Old Testament law in moving God's people to give. Avoiding lifeless legalism is a good thing, but something is very wrong with our notion of grace if these are the results.

Erwin McManus, pastor of a church in Southern California, tells the story of a man who was interested in joining their fellowship, but who was equally concerned that he not be asked to tithe. McManus retells the conversation:

> A middle-aged man sat down next to me and asked me a question that I knew was a setup: "Is this a grace church or a law church?" Sometimes all you can do is walk into the trap, so I answered, "This is a grace church." He responded with relief and said, "Good. I was concerned that you would require me to tithe."

I said, "Oh, no. We're definitely a grace church. The law says do not murder; grace says that we are not even to hate our enemies, but to love our enemies. The law says do not commit adultery; grace frees us even from having lust in our hearts for another man's wife. The law says to give 10 percent to tithe; grace says be generous. We would never stop you at 10 percent. You can give 20, 30, 40 percent of your income if you'd like."[86]

Since when did Jesus lower the bar? Remember His words in the Sermon on the Mount: "Unless your righteousness surpasses that of the Pharisees" (Matt 5:20). Grace is not an excuse to give less than the law requires. Its purpose is to empower us to go beyond what the law requires.

3.   When the tithe is a good starting point...

Jesus never equated tithing with the arrival point of stewardship. He calls us to join Peter, James, John, and Levi in *leaving everything*. He invites us to transfer the title of all our possessions into His name, and then stay on to manage the account. That's the real sign that your pocketbook has been baptized. But don't pretend you've taken the step of transferring the title if you're not at least giving what the Old and New Testaments refer to as the minimum standard of obedience. That's why tithing is a good starting point. It may be as much as you can give (and even more than you might think you can give), but it's where you need to begin if you're not already giving 10 percent of your income back to God.

I've been reflecting on the fact that 80 percent of the world's evangelical wealth resides in North America. I've also been pondering what could happen if Christians in North America raised their giving percentage to the Bible's minimum standard of a tithe. If this happened, it would result in an additional $140 billion a year for the work of Christ in the world. *$140 billion!* This would provide more than enough money to send a full-time missionary to every remaining unreached people group in the world. Think about it: we could actually finance the fulfillment of the Great Commission.

Perhaps today is the day to take the plunge—and begin tithing—as a way of taking that first step on the stewardship adventure.

Make All You Can, Save All You Can, Give All You Can

John Wesley coined the phrase, "Make all you can, save all you can, so that you can give away all you can."[87] Wesley lived that out in his own life, but he also encouraged those under his care to do the same. One of the results of his people's willingness to live this way with their money was a spiritual awakening that also impacted the social landscape of England and America. The early Methodists created educational and vocational opportunities for those who couldn't get them, lobbied for new child labor laws, and were the frontrunners in the fight against slavery. Their belief that God was in charge of all of their money went hand in hand with their ability to participate with Him in changing the world.

Toward the end of Wesley's life, though, he gave a prophetic warning. He predicted the Methodist movement would cease to experience revival when affluence found its way into his people's hearts. Wesley knew if his people began to settle for making and saving all they could, but failed to take seriously the charge to give it away, the Spirit's power and presence eventually would be quenched. Over time, that's precisely what happened. Second and third generation Methodists made a lot of money and saved their money, but they gave less and less money (proportionately) away. Correspondingly, the revival ceased.

Today, most of us within the Wesleyan tradition still appreciate our heritage and the convictions that drove our forefathers. Some of us still even preach about the gospel's power to change lives and transform whole communities. But that kind of transformation won't happen if the gospel doesn't radically affect our pocketbooks. The compartmentalization phenomenon of American Christianity has reduced the gospel to a means of getting to heaven. It's become a pie-in-the-sky religion that has little influence on the way we view and use money here on earth. The result of this compartmentalization is what Wesley predicted: *the power of God's Spirit to bring real transformation has been quenched in many of our churches.*

It reminds me of the great Catholic theologian Thomas Aquinas, who interrupted Pope Innocent II while he was counting a large sum of money. The Pope greeted Aquinas with the words, "You see, Thomas, the church can no longer say, 'Silver or gold have I none.'" Aquinas replied, "True, holy father, but neither can she now say, 'Rise and walk.'"

Levi, the Levite

Luke mentions Levi's name three times in the brief episode of Jesus calling him to be His disciple. When something gets mentioned three times in Scripture, it's intended to be a neon sign for readers to take notice. Levi's name has that kind of significance.

In the Old Testament there were twelve tribes that made up the people of Israel. It was the tribe of Levi that God called to be the spiritual leaders of His people:

> Levites, I am giving you the priesthood as a gift.
>
> —Num. 18:7

This gift of leadership came with a financial cost, though. God told the Levites they would receive no share in the land inheritance when Israel entered the Promised Land:

> You will have no inheritance in the land.
>
> —Num. 18:20a

This was neither metaphor nor hyperbole. It was the Levites' financial reality. They would make a living by serving God and ministering to the other eleven tribes of Israel. But their financial situation would be more vulnerable than that of their brothers and sisters. The fact that they wouldn't have an inheritance in the land would force them into a greater dependence upon God.

I wonder if any of the Levites felt shorted in this arrangement. After all, they had to wander around in the wilderness for forty years, just like the other tribes. They had to fight for the possession of the Promised Land, too. Yet when they got there, they received no share of the land. But God had His purposes for the Levites:

I will be your share and inheritance.

—Num. 18:20b

Basically, God was saying to the Levites, "You won't get any inheritance in the land, but the invitation to follow Me in this way is not to be viewed as burdensome. I want you to receive the priesthood as a gift. I want to reveal to you that I am your true Inheritance. I want to show you that I will take care of you, and that I am enough to satisfy you."

I will be your share and inheritance.

God was calling the Levites into a special relationship with Him, where they would become a living illustration for the rest of His people of what it looked like to play for an Audience of One with their resources.

Becoming Twenty-First Century Levites

Shortly after that night when Amanda and I transferred the title into Jesus' name, we embarked on a journey to Wilmore, Kentucky, in obedience to God's call on our lives. Amanda still had a year of college remaining, and I was just beginning seminary. We had only been married two weeks, and immediately we felt the pressure of how we were going to make it financially. The tuition bills and living expenses far exceeded our income and savings. But it was during this chapter of our marriage that we experienced what it meant for God to become our Inheritance. Perhaps more significant than any lesson I learned in my seminary classes was the lesson God wanted to teach us about becoming Levites.

The stories of God's provision filled up the pages of our prayer journals during those two-and-a-half years. I'll never forget the first story. Coming home from class one day during the beginning of the semester, I found Amanda crying on our bed. She had just received some discouraging news. The apartment complex we were moving into the following month was raising the rent by ten dollars a month. Ten dollars might not sound like a lot, but that's how tight things were. We sensed we were supposed to move, though, so we purposed to trust God for the additional ten dollars a month we needed. The next month, as we were signing the paperwork and giving the apartment manager our bank account information, she casually asked us, "Did I mention to you that you wouldn't be paying any rent?"

Our dropped jaws and raised eyebrows clearly communicated to her, *No, I think we would have remembered that little detail.*

"Oh, yes," she continued. "There is a clause in this apartment complex's rental agreement that whichever tenant is making the least amount of money does not have to pay any rent during that month."

It sounded too good to be true, but there really was such a clause in the apartment complex's rental agreement. She showed it to us. The manager wasn't finished, either: "I probably forgot to tell you that your utilities are free, too."

Amanda started crying right there in the apartment manager's office. This time, though, they were tears of joy. It was the first of many times when our eyes would be opened to the fact that God was our Inheritance, and He would provide what we needed in order to follow His call.

During those two-and-a-half years, we received over thirty-five thousand dollars of unexpected provision.

At the same time God was providing for us, though, He was also teaching us how to give away our money. God was reminding us that everything we had belonged to Him. And at times, He would prompt us to let what little we had slip through our fingers. It would have been easy to justify holding on to everything we got during those years. After all, we were the ones in need. However, God wanted to make sure we understood that the lesson of His provision and the lesson of letting it slip through our fingers went hand in hand. God never intends for us to separate His gracious provision from learning to give it away. It's the prosperity gospel that divides them.

Levi Lived Up to His Name

When Jesus called Levi to follow Him, essentially he was saying the same thing God had said to the tribe of Levi: "The priestly role I want you to play in My church is a gift. You will have no earthly inheritance, but I will be your inheritance."

As Levi got up from his tax collector's booth and left everything behind, in a very real sense he was living up to his name. He was becoming a Levite, exchanging his earthly inheritance of money for an eternal inheritance in God. As a result, he began throwing great banquets for Jesus with his newly redeemed money, and God's kingdom was getting advanced in his sphere of influence. Levi was becoming a Levite!

Imagine!

Imagine what would happen if we all lived up to our name as Levites? Perhaps you're thinking: *My name isn't Levi. I'm no Levite. In fact, I'm a Gentile!* The New Testament says there is a priesthood of *all* believers now. 1 Peter 2:5 and Revelation 1:6 plainly state that those who have said yes to following Jesus have become part of God's kingdom of priests. Translation: *We're all Levites!*

Just think if we all lived up to our name as Levi did. Imagine all the mega-banquets we could throw if the title of all our possessions was transferred into Jesus' name. Imagine the joy we would feel as we sense heaven smiling on us. Imagine what it would be like to actually experience God as our Inheritance as we learn to play for an Audience of One with our money!

Prayer of a Levite

Riches I heed not, nor man's empty praise,
Thou mine Inheritance, now and always;
Thou and Thou only, first in my heart,
High King of heaven, my Treasure, Thou art.[88]

—Be Thou My Vision (v3)

Going Deeper

1. If you have not yet become a Levite, make the decision to start following in Levi's footsteps today. Playing for an Audience of One with your money begins by transferring the title of all your money and your possessions into Jesus' name.
2. If you're not tithing, take the plunge. It's not the end goal of giving, but it's a good starting point. Writing that tithe check at the beginning of every month will remind you that all of your money belongs to God, and will help set the tone for the way you spend the other 90 percent during the rest of the month.
3. Ask God to give you a vision for something you can do to advance His kingdom in your sphere of influence, and then pray that He will make you rich *so that* you can be generous toward that vision. Remember: be careful what you pray for. God loves to answer this kind of prayer!
4. Begin a personal Good Samaritan Fund at home, setting aside an additional amount of money (above the tithe) each month, and earmarking it for needs God may bring across your path.
5. Use Christmas as an opportunity to throw a birthday party for Jesus rather than spreading the Affluenza bug. Get a *World Vision* or *Gospel for Asia* catalog and purchase gifts for the needy in the names of your family members and friends.
6. Prayerfully establish an entertainment budget and stick to it. Setting a budget will free you from feeling false guilt when you do something fun, but it will also provide parameters and accountability so you're not indulging in whatever you want whenever you want just because you have the financial means to do so.
7. If you want to go deeper on this topic, read *Money, Possessions, and Eternity* by Randy Alcorn.

Chapter 9

Playing for the Crowd

"I'm not sure which occupies the lower sphere,
he who hungers for money,
or he who thirsts for applause."[89]

—J. H. Jewett

SALLY FIELD WAS presented the Academy Award for best actress in 1979 for her inspiring portrayal of Norma Rae in the movie with the same name. Even that honor, though, was not enough to give her the sense that she had the esteem of her colleagues. In 1984, she was recognized again for her gutsy performance in *Places in the Heart*. But as she stepped up to the podium to collect her second Oscar and give her acceptance speech, she burst out with what obviously had been gnawing at her the past five years. Near tears, she gleefully confessed to the Academy, "I haven't had an orthodox career, and I've wanted more than anything to have your respect. The first time I didn't feel it, but this time I feel it, and I can't deny the fact that you like me, right now, you like me!"[90]

Millions of onlookers could relate to Sally's longing to be liked and her craving for her peers' approval. Few have the guts to be so transparent about it, though, especially on national television. Of course, the question remains: How long did her feelings of approval really last?

If winning the most prestigious acting award the first time didn't take care of her agonizing sense of inadequacy, would winning it again really make a long-term difference?

Achievement is no lasting antidote to the craving for more affirmation. In fact, it is frequently those who obtain some measure of greatness who continue to strive the most after the accolades and applause of others. Like J. Paul Getty and his quest for getting just a little more money, many people are ruled by the tyranny of getting just a little bit more approval. Our thirst for approval will never be satisfied, though, as long as we're looking for it to be quenched by other human beings. Once the initial high of the approval fix wears off, we will be left feeling empty again. "Preoccupation with success deprives us of rest —always climb a little higher and get a little more…we worry about our image and our reputation until we have no rest."[91]

Living for the approval of the crowd not only keeps us from experiencing the joy and purpose of playing for an Audience of One. Eventually, it destroys us.

God's Gracious Warning to Me

Frequently, God's Word is meant to inspire us with hope and vision. Often times, it encourages us to persevere. At other points, it instructs us. But sometimes, its purpose is to warn us, to paint a picture of what will happen if we refuse to heed God's voice. The story of King Saul is one of those gracious warnings, particularly for those who struggle with the inclination to seek after the approval of others. What makes the story such a tragedy is the potential for what Saul could have become if it were not for the people-pleasing tendency that ultimately dominated his life.

God has brought me back to King Saul's story again and again whenever I find myself drifting toward playing for the crowd rather than playing for Him. It's not a hellfire and brimstone message. Rather, I've come to hear it as a gracious warning to my soul, one that reminds me of the cost of going the way of people pleasing. If you've ever found yourself in a similar drifting pattern, my prayer is this story will become God's gracious warning to you, too.

"Like All the Other Nations"

Saul's story began at a very significant point in Israel's history. For several centuries leading up to Saul's reign, the Hebrew people were a nation under God's kingship. They had no earthly king. There was no president or prime minister presiding over the nation. God was her King. Eventually, though, the people of Israel complained about this arrangement. They wanted an earthly king to rule over them, and they began insisting on it. The prophet Samuel tried to talk Israel out of pursuing this plan, but they were obstinate:

> The people refused to listen to Samuel. "No!" they said. "We want a king over us. Then we will be like all the other nations."
>
> —1 Sam. 8:19

Samuel took this rebuff personally, but it was God who was the real object of Israel's rejection:

> It is not you they have rejected...they have rejected Me as their King.
>
> —1 Sam. 8:7

In spite of Israel's rejection, God accommodated their desire for a king. But He only did so on one condition: *He* would select their king. And as is God's custom, the person He had in mind for the job was not someone who was looking for it.

Saul was an unassuming, unpretentious, unsophisticated man. He worked on the family farm, helping his father take care of the donkeys. He wasn't exactly being groomed for the throne. He didn't look at all like one of the other nations' kings. In fact, when the prophet Samuel relayed God's message to Saul that he was to be the first king, he replied:

> But am I not a Benjamite, from the smallest tribe of Israel, and is not my clan the least of all the clans of the tribe of Benjamin? Why do you say such a thing to me?
>
> —1 Sam. 9:21

Saul wasn't looking to be king. He was content to go on helping take care of his father's donkey farm. Of course, this is precisely the kind of raw material that God has always used to accomplish His purposes. He had dealt with Saul's type before:

- Abraham and Sarah didn't start out as the father and mother of the faith. They laughed at God when He promised them a child in their old age.
- Moses didn't start out as the valiant leader of a million Hebrews. He dragged his feet for quite a while before finally being willing to leave the familiarity of his desert shepherd's post.
- Gideon didn't start out as the brave military leader. He put out not one but two fleece tests before he trusted God enough to obey.

Saul seemed to be cut from the same cloth as these heroes of the faith.

God's Forewarning to Saul

Insecurity and inadequacy didn't disqualify Saul from being God's selection for king. The only criterion for Israel's first king was someone who would obey. God was so desirous of an obedient king that He gave Saul a heads-up about a future event where he would be tempted to disobey. The forewarning was this: there would be a moment when Saul would find himself in a military pinch at Gilgal. Once there he would need to remember and obey this command:

> You must wait seven days until I [Samuel] come to you and tell you what you are to do.
>
> —1 Sam. 10:8

That was the one command God gave Saul to obey. Remember it, because it will come up later in the story.

Grace for the Humble

When it came time for Saul's inauguration as king, Samuel called together all the people of Israel for the coronation. It was a beautiful ceremony, except for one minor glitch. While Saul was being pronounced king, he was nowhere to be found. As Samuel inquired of the Lord as to his whereabouts, it was revealed:

> He [Saul] has hidden himself among the baggage.
>
> —1 Sam. 10:22

Try to imagine this scene in our modern-day political context: the newly elected president of the United States of America being so sheepish that he would actually hide from the limelight when it was announced he was to be the next commander in chief! The fact that Saul was hiding among the baggage did not exactly instill confidence among some of his constituents. No wonder there were people in Israel who were skeptical of God's selection of their first king:

> Some troublemakers said, "How can this fellow save us?" They despised him and brought him no gifts. But Saul kept silent.
>
> —1 Sam. 10:27

Saul kept silent because he didn't want the spotlight. He wasn't looking for applause from the crowd. He didn't "need" to be the king. Like Abraham, Moses, and Gideon, he wrestled with insecurity issues. But early on in his life, as Samuel would later say of him, Saul was appropriately "small in his own eyes" (1 Sam. 15:17). That's why he began his reign so well. As James says, "God opposes the proud, but gives grace to the humble" (4:6).

Saul's humility opened up the floodgates through which God's help could flow. His first act as king was to rescue the city of Jabesh from one of Israel's enemies, the Ammonites. More significant than Saul's military victory, though, was how he handled the potentially divisive situation following the win. After leading Israel to a great victory on the battlefield, his approval rating skyrocketed. Those who had been his supporters from the beginning of his reign began to voice their convictions about what to do with those troublemakers who had questioned his kingship back at the inauguration ceremony. Their plan was simple:

> Bring these men to us and we will put them to death.
>
> —1 Sam. 11:12

Saul could have gone along with this plan. Nobody, except for God, would have even blinked an eye. This was what the kings of the other nations did all the time to those who dared question the legitimacy of their claim to the throne. Killing dissenters was a very efficient way for the king to keep his public approval rating high. You didn't see "Question Authority" attached to the bumpers of very many wagons in those days. But Saul refused to respond to his dissenters like the kings of all of the other nations. Instead, he replied:

> No one shall be put to death today, for this day the Lord has rescued Israel.
>
> —1 Sam. 11:13

He immediately gave credit to the Lord for the victory on the battlefield. Saul refused to use this win as leverage for propping up his own reputation among the people. In fact, he didn't even rub his dissenters' noses in it. He took the high road, using the win on the battlefield as an opportunity to cast vision for what the Lord had done. I probably would have been tempted to use the victory to vindicate myself, but Saul used it as an opportunity to establish unity among all of Israel.

Abraham Lincoln faced a similar temptation at the conclusion of the Civil War. Many northerners wanted harsher retribution to be meted out against the South. Lincoln had legitimate reasons to indulge these vengeful feelings. The South had so rejected his authority that they actually elected their own president, Jefferson Davis. But Lincoln refused to pursue a path of vengeance after the war was over. He knew what the fragile nation really needed was a larger vision that would unite both sides. Winning the Civil War wasn't about vindication for Lincoln. It wasn't about him at all. For Lincoln, winning the war was about bringing the Union back together. There was no need to rub the South's nose in the victory.

Saul took this same high road. He knew the win wasn't about him. At least at this point in the story, he was still appropriately small in his own eyes. Unfortunately, it was all down hill from here for Saul.

Waiting Is the Hardest Thing to Do

Two years into his reign, Saul found himself on the cusp of a battle against the Philistines, and stationed at Gilgal. Remember Gilgal? This was the test for which God was preparing Saul. This was the precise situation about which God had warned him through the prophet Samuel:

> Go down ahead of me to Gilgal. I [Samuel] will surely come down to you
> to sacrifice burnt offerings, but you must wait seven days *until I come
> to you* and tell you what you are to do.
>
> —1 Sam. 10:8, emphasis mine

God had set up a strict protocol when it came to who could offer up the pre-battle sacrifices. Not just anyone could do it. It was the prophet-priest alone who was appointed to perform this task. Even the king wasn't allowed to play this role. No matter what, Saul was supposed to wait for Samuel before he made a military move.

God's reminder to wait for the prophet before going into battle wouldn't have been a surprise to Saul. He knew this was how it worked. In fact, when Saul was given this command to wait (two years earlier), he probably thought, *No problem, I'll wait for Samuel. That's what I'm always supposed to do before a battle. Why are you giving me so much warning on this one, Lord?*

Once the military scenario began to unfold, though, Saul understood the reason for God's forewarning:

> The Philistines assembled to fight Israel, with three thousand chariots,
> six thousand charioteers, and soldiers as numerous as the sand on the
> seashore....When the men of Israel saw that their situation was critical

and that their army was hard pressed, they hid in caves and thickets, among the rocks, and in pits and cisterns.…Saul remained at Gilgal, and all the troops with him were quaking with fear. He waited seven days, the time set by Samuel; but Samuel did not come to Gilgal, *and Saul's men began to scatter.*

—1 Sam. 13:5-8, emphasis mine

Try to get this scene in your mind: there is a massive constituency of the Philistine army assembled and ready to fight. Meanwhile, Saul's army is hiding and quaking with fear. Things go from bad to worse when his soldiers begin to scatter. As the commander in chief, Saul had a decision to make: keep waiting for Samuel, or take action before his military position was further compromised.

We're told, "He waited seven days, the time set by Samuel." This was not a description of full obedience, though. It was simply the narrator's way of pointing out that this was the test about which God had warned Saul at the beginning of his reign. But remember the details of the command. It wasn't just that Saul needed to wait until the *seventh* day. The directive was more precise than that: Saul had been ordered to wait the *whole* seven days—specifically, to wait *until Samuel came.*

Given the situation in which Saul found himself, it's not difficult to imagine the agony he felt waiting for Samuel's arrival. It's tough to wait and do nothing when your world seems to be falling apart.

Henri Nouwen shares a lesson he learned from some trapeze artists regarding the difficulty of waiting:

There is a special relationship between the flyer and the catcher.…As the flyer is swinging high above the crowd, the moment comes when he lets go of the trapeze, when he arcs out into the air. For that moment, which must feel like an eternity, the flyer is suspended in nothingness. It is too late to reach back for the trapeze. There is no going back now. However, it is too soon to be grasped by the one who will catch him. He cannot accelerate the catch. In that moment, his job is to be as still and motionless as he can.

"The flyer must never try to catch the catcher," the trapeze artist told me. "He must wait in absolute trust. The catcher will catch him.

But he must wait. His job is not to flail about in anxiety. In fact, if he does, it could kill him. His job is to be still. To wait. And to wait is the hardest work of all."[92]

Saul was doing the hard work of waiting. And to his credit, he had waited until the seventh day. How could he be expected to wait any longer? He was already in a vulnerable position. Once his soldiers started scattering, it only exposed his military weakness that much more.

Put yourself in Saul's shoes. The enemy is pressing in on you, your men are hiding, others are quaking with fear, some are beginning to scatter, and the few soldiers who remain with you are looking for you to do something. And yet you know your orders: *you are to wait until Samuel arrives before you make a move.*

What would you do?

At one of those defining moments when you find out what you're really made of, Saul made his decision. He literally grabbed the bull by the horns and took matters into his own hands:

> Saul's men began to scatter. So he said, "Bring me the burnt offering."
>
> —1 Sam. 13:9

In a lot of leadership circles, Saul would be held up here as a master improviser, someone who knew how to get things done, an emotionally intelligent leader with a clear pulse on what his subordinates were thinking and feeling. Saul knew what he needed to do to keep the men on his team. Some would argue that Saul was just doing the necessary "course correcting" to relieve his men of their fears and get them back on the battlefield. From a utilitarian standpoint, offering the sacrifice looked like a brilliant tactical move that could help restore the troops' morale.

But from God's perspective, Saul buckled under the pressure of his men. The anxiety Saul felt watching his soldiers scatter was too much for him to bear, so he did something to alleviate the discomfort. Even though Saul knew what God had called him to do, the prospect of losing his men's support was more than he could take. So he prepared the burnt offering. You can probably guess what happened next:

> Just as he finished making the offering, Samuel arrived.
>
> —1 Sam. 13:10

What makes this story such a tragedy is that Saul almost made it. He waited until the seventh day, but he didn't wait the *whole* seven days. When Samuel arrived and questioned him as to why he didn't wait, Saul gave his feeble defense:

> When I saw that the men were scattering...I felt compelled to offer the burnt offering.
>
> —1 Sam. 13:11-12

Saul's own words indicted him. He admitted he had been more attentive to his men than to the word of God. As H.G. Wells said, "The trouble with so many people is that the voice of their neighbors sounds louder in their ears than the voice of God."[93]

The Price Tag for Playing for the Crowd

Saul let the fear, pressure, and voices of those around him dictate what he did, and it cost him the legacy of his kingdom:

> "You acted foolishly," Samuel said. "You have not kept the command the Lord your God gave you; if you had, He would have established your kingdom over Israel for all time. But now your kingdom will not endure; the Lord has sought out a man after His own heart."
>
> —1 Sam. 13:13-14

The price tag for Saul's disobedience was costly. All because he felt compelled to respond to his men's voices rather than the voice of the One who had clearly spoken to him. This tells us how serious God considers disobedience that is motivated by listening to our neighbor's voices.

If Saul had just waited a little longer, his future would have looked very different.

The Marshmallow Test

The ability to wait is often the distinguishing mark among those who make it in life, as documented by the following study. Author Daniel Goleman sets the stage:

> Just imagine you're four years old, and someone makes the following proposal: If you'll wait until he runs an errand, you can have two marshmallows for a treat. If you can't wait until then, you can only have one—but you can have it right now.[94]

This marshmallow test was actually performed on some four-year-old children of Stanford University faculty during the 1960's. The results were fascinating. There were some four-year-olds who were able to wait fifteen to twenty minutes for the experimenters to return from their "errand." In order for these preschoolers to maintain their patient waiting and so gain the two marshmallow reward, they would do all sorts of things to distract themselves from giving in to the temptation of grabbing the one marshmallow: cover their eyes, sing, talk to themselves, and play games with their hands and feet. Some even tried to go to sleep to pass the time. In the end, these were the four-year-olds who got the two marshmallows.

Then there were the more impulsive children, those who grabbed the one marshmallow, usually within seconds of it being placed within their reach.

The researchers performing this study then tracked down both sets of four-year-olds as they were graduating from high school. Goleman reports what they found:

> The emotional and social difference between the grab-the-marshmallow preschooler and their gratification-delaying peers was dramatic. Those who resisted temptation at four were now, as adolescents, more socially competent: personally effective, self-assertive, and better able to cope with the frustrations of life. They were less likely to go to pieces, freeze, or regress under stress, or become rattled and disorganized when pressured; they embraced challenges and pursued them instead of giving up even in the face of difficulties.[95]

On the other hand, those who grabbed the one marshmallow tended to be stubborn and easily upset by frustrations. They thought of themselves as "bad" or unworthy, they were prone to jealousy and anger, and as a whole they generally overreacted to irritations. And fourteen years later, they were still giving in to their desires for instant gratification.

The clincher in this study, though, was the relationship between delayed gratification and SAT scores. The way children responded to this test of delayed gratification was twice as powerful a predictor of what their SAT scores would be than an IQ test. *Those who waited the longest for the two marshmallows had an average SAT score 210 points higher than those who grabbed the one marshmallow!*

Saul grabbed the one marshmallow. It brought him immediate gratification, too. But it didn't last. In fact, the very thing he had hoped would save his life actually brought the death of his long-term future. That's what happens when we choose the one marshmallow.

When the People Around Us "Scatter"

Soon after responding to God's nudge to read Saul's story, a number of people in our church began to scatter. I say, "scatter," because their actions paralleled what Saul's soldiers were doing on that hill in Gilgal. People were calling me up late at night or showing up at my office to inform me there were families in our fellowship who were ready to leave. Evidently, our church wasn't doing enough to "meet their needs." No pastor likes to hear these kinds of reports. The common denominator in all of these conversations was a feeling of panic. And there was an expectation that once I heard about the so-called problems, I would respond to the "scattering" right then and there.

The issues that people wanted addressed varied: a service for those desiring a deeper worship experience, a college age ministry for those threatening to go across town to a church that offered such a program. Others were concerned that our teenagers were ready to "flee" (that was actually the word used) to a more exciting youth group if we didn't make some changes *now*.

Our church does not typically spend a lot of energy in panic mode, trying to micromanage what the leadership should be doing. But for whatever reason, there was a fearful sense of the future that crept into the air. Let me be the first to admit that I was very tempted to take some immediate steps to "raise the morale of the troops" (read: alleviate my own anxiety and make the people happy). But I knew the changes these people were advocating were not from God. The Lord had given the leadership a clear course to pursue with regard to our future. So the test for me was whether I would stay true to it or not.

I cannot underscore how badly I was tempted to "solve the morale problem" when the scattering began. It would have brought immediate satisfaction to those wanting something to be done. It also would have brought relief to me. I wouldn't have had to deal with people's disapproval and my own feelings that I was failing as a leader. There were diplomatic decisions I could have made that would have made everyone happier with me. *Everyone but God.*

In the end, I waited. It's not that I did nothing during this season when people were "scattering." I had plenty of vision-casting conversations. I did my best to help people see the big picture of what we were trying to do. I just didn't do what they wanted me to do *when* they wanted me to do it. And eventually, the anxiety died down. Several months later, we began to move ahead with the ministry plans we sensed God calling us to pursue. Shortly thereafter, there was confirmation as to why we were supposed to wait. The Lord rewarded our willingness not to react out of panic with a greater measure of His anointing on our ministry. To be honest, though, I don't get any of the credit for waiting. I wouldn't have waited if God hadn't nudged me to read Saul's story right before the "scattering" began. This story was fresh in my mind when the test came. It really did serve as a gracious warning to me.

The Price Tag for Not Playing for the Crowd

The character flaw that tripped up Saul is one that trips up many people. There is, in just about all of us, an insidious temptation to listen to the crowd's voice (or perhaps to specific voices within the crowd) more than to the voice of the One who really matters. The fear of disapproval, criticism, and failure compels us to tune in to those whose opinions we think will make the difference in our wellbeing. Our fear is not without reason. People's opinions of us can impact our future. There is a price tag for not playing for the crowd. There always has been.

Aleksandr Solzhenitsyn tells the story of what happened in 1938 to one Russian who swam up stream against the flow of the crowd:

> A district party conference was under way in Moscow Province. It was presided over by a new secretary of the District Party Committee, replacing one recently arrested. At the conclusion of the conference, a tribute to Comrade Stalin was called for. Of course, everyone stood up (just as everyone had leaped to his feet during the conference with every mention of his name). The hall echoed with 'stormy applause, rising to an ovation.' For three minutes, four minutes, five minutes, the 'stormy applause, rising to an ovation,' continued. But palms were getting sore and raised arms were already aching. And the older people were panting from exhaustion. It was becoming insufferably silly even to those who adored Stalin. However, who would dare to be the first to stop? The secretary of the District Party could have done it. He was standing on the platform, and it was he who had just called for the ovation. But he was a newcomer. He had taken the place of a man who'd been arrested. He was afraid! After all, NKVD men were standing in the hall applauding and watching to see who would quit first!

> The director of the local paper factory, an independent and strong-minded man, stood with the presidium. Aware of all the falsity and all the impossibility of the situation, he still kept on applauding! Nine minutes! Ten! In anguish he watched the secretary of the District Party committee, but the latter dared not stop. Insanity! To the last man! With make-believe enthusiasm on their faces, looking at each other with faint hope, the district leaders were just going to go on and on applauding till they fell where they stood, till they were carried out of the hall on stretchers! And even those who were left would not falter....Then, after eleven minutes, the director of the paper factory assumed a businesslike expression and sat down in his seat. And, oh, a miracle took place! Where had the universal, uninhibited, indescribable enthusiasm gone?

To a man, everyone else stopped dead and sat down....That, however, was how they discovered who the independent people were. And that was how they went about eliminating them. That same night the factory director was arrested. They easily pasted ten years on him on the pretext of something quite different. But after he had signed Form 206, the final document of the interrogation, his interrogator reminded him: "Don't ever be the first to stop applauding!"[96]

The question is not whether we will we pay a price for going *against* the crowd. We almost certainly will. The real question is whether the price tag for doing so will be less costly than the one attached to playing *for* the crowd. Saul lost the legacy of his kingdom because he thought playing for an Audience of One was too high a price to pay. The tragic irony is that if he had stayed true to God's voice, he actually would have secured the legacy of the kingdom of Israel forever. I'm sure Samuel's words haunted him the rest of his life: "Saul, if you would have obeyed, I would have established your kingdom over Israel for all time."

Resolve

God was looking to build a dynasty with a king who would be willing to stand up and say, *Despite the discomfort of watching all three thousand of my soldiers scatter, I'm not moving. I don't care how many Philistines I have to face. Even if I'm the only one left standing on this hill at the end of the day, so be it!*

God is still looking for this kind of resolve today. There are times in life when He tests our mettle to find out if we're willing to obey His voice amidst all those voices that would persuade us to go another way. It's not that we need to go seeking after spiritual lone ranger opportunities. We simply need to obey God if and when those around us "scatter." Regardless of how desperate our situation seems, or what people are saying about us, or how lonely we feel, we are to keep our ears attuned to the voice of the Audience of One.

My resolve has become stronger as I've considered the truth behind one of Philip Yancey's growing aspirations: "My goal for growing older, for preparing to die is to care less about how others view me and more about how God views me. We'll have much longer together, after all."[97]

A Second Chance

Despite the fact that Saul had lost the legacy of an enduring kingdom, God wasn't finished with him yet. God gave him another opportunity to pass the test of listening to His voice amidst the competing voices of his men. Saul's second chance to obey was no more complicated than the first:

> Totally destroy the Amalekites.
>
> —1 Sam. 15:3

In order to grasp the meaning of this command, it's important to understand the term "totally destroy." It wasn't so much a military phrase as it was a religious one. A more literal translation of this phrase is "to irrevocably give over to the Lord." It means to completely consecrate something to God. Totally destroying the Amalekites was not primarily about killing them (though they were to be killed) as much as it was about sacrificing all of the spoils of victory to God.

This kind of "destroying" was an absolutely countercultural approach to war. The primary reason for attacking another nation then (as it often is today) was to acquire possessions: land, slaves, livestock, and treasure. But God was asking Saul to sacrifice all of the potential spoils of war to Him in an act of worship. Yes, Israel was serving as God's instrument for punishing the wicked Amalekites, but judgment wasn't the primary point of the command for Saul. The real issue for Saul was whether he would sacrifice everything to God or use this war as a means of making a profit—like all the other kings did when they won a battle.

Here's what he did:

> Then Saul attacked the Amalekites....He took Agag king of the Amalekites alive, and all of his people he totally destroyed with the sword. But Saul and the army spared Agag and the best of the sheep

and cattle...everything that was good. These they were unwilling
to destroy completely, but everything that was despised and weak
they totally destroyed.

—1 Sam. 15:7-9

Try to imagine this scene from God's perspective: Saul and his army
kept the best of the livestock for themselves, and totally destroyed only
that which was *despised and weak*. In other words, Saul gave God the
dregs, the leftovers, the hand-me-downs.

It reminds me of the time a newly married couple recycled one of
their unwanted wedding gifts at their friends' wedding. There's even
a name today for this kind of thing: "re-gifting." Unfortunately, they
forgot a critical step before rewrapping the gift. As their friends were
unwrapping the present, the "re-gifting" couple realized they had
forgotten to take their own nametag off the gift! You can imagine what
their friends thought about receiving that kind of present.

God doesn't want that kind of gift, either. In Malachi 1, He
says,

When you bring blind animals for sacrifice, is that not wrong? When
you sacrifice crippled animals, is that not wrong? Try offering them
to your governor! Would he be pleased with you? When you bring
injured, crippled, or diseased animals and offer them as sacrifices,
should I accept them from your hands? Cursed is the cheat who has
an acceptable male in his flock and vows to give it, but then sacrifices
a blemished animal to the Lord.

—Mal. 1:8, 13-14

Playing for Trophies, Parades, and Statues

Not only did Saul let his soldiers keep the best booty for themselves,
he also spared Agag, the king of the Amalekites. Why would he spare
the life of the opposing king? It was common practice in the ancient
near east for the victorious king to capture the defeated king alive and
make him a personal royal slave. That's what Saul was doing. Even
though God had commanded that everyone and everything associated
with the Amalekites be "totally" destroyed, Saul saw an opportunity

to advance his reputation by making King Agag his own personal trophy. He knew this would boost his image among the people of Israel. It probably did.

After the victory over the Amalekites, Saul led his troops (and King Agag) into Gilgal for a tickertape parade. Why Gilgal? Because Gilgal was where Saul's earlier act of disobedience had brought reproach from the prophet Samuel. It was the place where Saul was humiliated with the news he had lost the kingdom dynasty. Saul was going back to Gilgal in order to parade around his royal slave, King Agag! Agag was Saul's symbol of military strength. In other words, Saul was using the victory on the battlefield, not as an opportunity for worship and sacrifice, but as a way of exalting himself among the people of Israel. In fact, on the way to Gilgal, Saul made a brief pit stop in Carmel for the sole purpose of "setting up a monument in his own honor" (1 Sam. 15:12).

It's amazing what some of us will do for a few more ego strokes. One man, appropriately nicknamed "Cannonball," rationalized the reason he did what he did. When asked by a newspaper journalist why he had endured being blasted out of a cannon 1,200 times, the man replied, "Do you know what it's like to feel the applause of 60,000 people? That's why I did it!"[98]

While Saul was still posing for his statue, God commissioned Samuel to take him his pink slip as the king of Israel. When Samuel arrived, Saul played it cool, proclaiming he had totally destroyed everything, just as the Lord had asked him. Samuel's response to Saul's cover-up was classic:

> What then is this bleating of sheep in my ears? What is this lowing of cattle that I hear?
>
> —1 Sam. 15:14

Samuel didn't need to be Old Mac Donald to know what a "moo-moo" here and a "baa-baa" there meant. It meant not everything had been totally destroyed! Saul was caught red-handed. But instead of coming clean, he tried to argue his way out of it. He justified that the reason he had spared some of the spoils of war was in order to sacrifice them to God in a special worship service. Samuel was again the messenger of God's judgment against Saul:

> Does the Lord delight in burnt offerings and sacrifices as much as in obeying the voice of the Lord? To obey is better than sacrifice.... Because you have rejected the word of the Lord, He has rejected you as king.
>
> —1 Sam. 15:22-23

God's verdict finally provoked Saul to get honest about why he did what he did:

> Then Saul said to Samuel, "I have sinned. I violated the Lord's command and your instructions. I was afraid of the people and so I gave in to them"
>
> —1 Sam. 15:24

Just like Saul's earlier act of disobedience, it was his *fear of the people* that compelled him to give into their pleas to take some of the booty. As the ancient proverb says, "The fear of man will prove to be a snare" (Prov. 29:25). That snare kept squeezing the life out of Saul. He had already lost the legacy of a never-ending kingdom. Now it was costing him the crown. More accurately, it was costing him the anointing of God that came with the crown. For all intents and purposes, Saul's kingship was over. He retained the throne, but only because his grasp for power allowed him to hold onto it until God was ready to usher in the next king: David, a man after His own heart.

Exchanging One's Soul for the Applause of our Neighbors

What's so heartbreaking about the end of Saul's story is that he still was not as much concerned about his relationship to God as he was about securing for himself the affections, admiration, and applause of the people of Israel. Although Saul made what sounded like a genuine confession of sin, his real motive for doing so was to save face with the people. Perhaps the most tragic part of the story is the final interaction between Saul and Samuel. Even when Saul had nothing more to lose, except his soul, we see how bound he had become to playing for the crowd. His final request of Samuel said it all:

> I have sinned. But please honor me before the elders of my people and before Israel; come back with me, so that I may worship the Lord your God.
>
> —1 Sam. 15:30

Saul had become a full-fledged approval addict. He wasn't concerned about worshiping God anymore. He only wanted Samuel to join him so it would look like he had the religious establishment's endorsement. Even after forfeiting his kingdom legacy and losing God's anointing upon his kingship, Saul still could think only about one thing: "What will people think about me?" The prospect of losing face with his men was unbearable. It was the kind of suffering he was unwilling to endure. This price was too high to pay for Saul, even when he compared it to the value of his own soul.

That's how desperate Saul had become for his next approval fix. That's why he built a monument to himself at Carmel. That's why he wanted to parade around King Agag as his own personal trophy in Gilgal. That's why he begged Samuel to come back with him to worship the Lord. Each of these was just another attempt to promote his reputation among the people of Israel.

Saul never did detox from his addiction to people's approval. He spent the rest of his life trying to get a little bit more of it. His final years as king simply became a delivery system for gaining the honor and esteem of the people. Like most drugs, Saul's addiction to people's applause caused him to seek after a little bigger hit each time. When he didn't get it, he was restless and discontent. When he did, it never really lasted. And there was always something or someone standing between him and his next fix.

The primary obstacle to Saul being able to maintain his approval addiction habit was David, a man after God's own heart (1 Sam. 13:14). Ironically, David's focus was on pleasing God, and yet he ended up gaining the respect and admiration of the people. He didn't have to try to get it; it just came. After David killed Goliath, the people of Israel wrote a new song:

Saul has slain his thousands, and David his tens of thousands.

—1 Sam. 18:7

Scripture doesn't tell us what David thought about the song. Most likely he didn't think about it all. It's not that David had a *low* opinion of himself. He had *no* opinion of himself. As Brennan Manning writes of people like David, they are "neither overly sensitive to criticism nor inflated by praise, they recognize their brokenness, acknowledge their gifts, and refuse to take themselves seriously."[99]

On the other hand, Saul took himself very seriously. He thought about this song a lot! He was not particularly impressed with the lyrics of this little ditty either. After all, it's excruciatingly difficult for an approval addict to get a fix when the crowd is chanting someone else's name. Saul's response to this song provides a glimpse into what would dominate the rest of his life:

Saul was very angry; this refrain galled him. "They have credited David with tens of thousands," he thought, "but me with only thousands. What more can he get but the kingdom?" And from that time on Saul kept a jealous eye on David.

—1 Sam. 18:8-9

Saul's demise into playing for the crowd took complete control ✗ of him. His life orbited around the planets of pride, fear, jealousy, and an obsession with what people thought about him. He launched an all-out effort to find and kill David. His jealousy nearly moved him to murder his son Jonathan after he discovered that the allegiance of his own flesh and blood was with David. Perhaps Saul's darkest hour, though, came when he murdered eighty-five priests in cold blood. Why would he do such a ghastly thing? He was paranoid that the priests had sided with David.

It takes a lot of time and energy to try and control what everyone thinks about us.

Narcissism's Final Resting Place

Saul's story ended, appropriately, on the battlefield, on the very playing field where he had tried so hard to gain the people of Israel's applause. But it wasn't the sword of his enemies that ended his life. Saul fell on his own sword, a fitting analogy for his spiritual journey, which had become so narcissistic that it ultimately destroyed him.

J.H. Jewett says, "I'm not sure which occupies the lower sphere, he who hungers for money, or he who thirsts for applause."[100] Saul's thirst for applause cost him the legacy of a kingdom, the anointing and blessing of God on his reign, and eventually, his very life. In exchange, Saul got to live captive to pride, fear, and jealousy. As a bonus, he got to live under the gavel of the opinions of the people he was meant to lead. Not a great trade.

The Antidote to the People-Pleasing Disease

So what about us? How are we going to respond to the tragic warnings inherent within Saul's story? How do we play for an Audience of One when we find ourselves inclined to follow in Saul's footsteps? What is the antidote to this insidious temptation within most of us to play for the approval of others? A.W. Tozer writes:

> Artificiality is one curse that will drop away the moment we kneel at Jesus' feet and surrender ourselves to His meekness. Then we will not care what people think of us so long as God is pleased.…The rest He [Christ] offers is the rest of meekness, the blessed relief which comes when we accept ourselves for what we are and cease to pretend.[101]

God's deep desire for us is that we grow to become content in being children of our heavenly Father. He longs for us to stop playing for the affections and approval of our neighbors even more than we want to stop doing so. God is inviting us to experience the kind of rest that comes when we 'remain small in our own eyes.'

Becoming meek doesn't happen overnight. But unless you deal with your inclination to play for the crowd, it will eat away at your soul and make you hollow. Your perspective of yourself should be like that of Samuel Brengle, who, when introduced as "the great Doctor Brengle," later wrote in his journal:

If I appear great in his eyes, the Lord is most graciously helping me to see how absolutely nothing I am without Him, and helping me to keep little in my own eyes. He does use me. But...the axe cannot boast of the trees it has cut down. It could do nothing but for the woodsman. He made it, he sharpened it, and he used it. The moment he throws it aside, it becomes only old iron. O that I may never lose sight of this.[102]

Saul's reign began well because he was appropriately "small in his own eyes." The key, it seems to me, is to stay this way throughout life's journey.

Prayer of Meekness

"Lord, make me childlike. Deliver me from the urge to compete with another for place or prestige or position. I would be simple and artless as a little child. Deliver me from pose and pretense. Forgive me for thinking of myself. Help me to forget myself and find my true peace in beholding You."[103]

—A.W. Tozer

Going Deeper

1. Read the story of Saul in its entirety (1 Sam. 8–31). Allow the gracious warnings in this story to attune your ears to the One to whom you want to listen and obey.
2. Pray for and practice meekness, accepting yourself for who you are and "ceasing to pretend." Fire yourself from the job of trying to manage everyone's opinion of you.
3. Look for a way to shower someone you envy with glowing words, praise, or credit. Figuratively speaking, write a song about that person—even if it feels like it might decrease your stock value to the people who hear the song.
4. The transitional verse that marks the end of Saul's anointing and the beginning of David's is 1 Samuel 16:7. Memorize this verse as a way of marking the end of your days playing for the crowd:

The Lord does not look at the things man looks at. Man looks at the outward appearance, but the Lord looks at the heart.

—1 Sam. 16:7

Chapter 10

HOBBLING TOWARD HOLINESS

*"The saints are those who hobble toward holiness
with an insatiable thirst for God."[104]*
—Elliot Wright

IN ORDER TO compete in the Olympic Trials marathon, Beth Anne
DeCiantis needed to complete the twenty-seven-mile course in less than
two hours and forty-five minutes. *Runner's World* tells the nail-biting
story of her attempt to qualify:

> Beth started strong but began having trouble around mile twenty-three.
> She reached the final straightaway at 2:43, with just two minutes left
> to qualify. Two hundred yards from the finish, she stumbled and fell.
> Dazed, she stayed down for twenty seconds. The clock was ticking:
> 2:44, less than a minute to go.
>
> Beth Anne staggered to her feet and began walking. Five yards short of
> the finish, with ten seconds to go, she fell again. She began to crawl,
> the crowd cheering her on, and crossed the finish line on her hands
> and knees. Her time? 2:44:57.[105]

This story illustrates something about the spiritual life. It's a
reminder that just because you start out playing for an Audience of One

does not mean you won't fall at points during the journey. You will. The real issue is whether you will keep going after you fall—even if you have to crawl on your hands and knees to get to the finish line.

The Pitfalls of Pursuing Holiness

You are making a fatal mistake if your aspiration to play for an Audience of One is predicated on the notion that once you embark on the journey, you'll never blow it again. Not only will this goal set you up for disappointment when you do fall short, it will keep you fixated on yourself rather than on God. Self-evaluation can be a helpful tool in your walk with God, but if your objective is to be sinless, you will become Narcissus on your knees. You will find yourself constantly gazing into the pool of your own reflection in order to assess your spiritual condition. Oswald Chambers writes, "A saint is never consciously a saint—a saint is consciously dependent on God."[106]

John Wesley is often cited as one who claimed that a form of Christian perfection was possible to attain here on earth. But even his version of perfection was no absolute perfection. Wesley taught that Christians who had fully surrendered themselves to God could still fall back into willful sin. He also warned that even completely yielded Christians would sometimes commit what he termed *sins of infirmity*—wrongdoings that result from spiritual ignorance or a lack of discernment.

Let's face it: it doesn't matter how serious we are about playing for an Audience of One. There is no way, on this side of heaven, to be completely free from sin or its effects. That is why striving after absolute perfection is so damaging to our pursuit of a God-honoring, soul-satisfying walk. It causes us to miss the point of what living wholly for God is all about. As Oswald Chambers warns:

> It is a trap to presume that God wants to make us perfect specimens of what He can do....The emphasis of holiness movements tends to be that God is producing specimens of holiness to put in His museum. If you accept this concept of personal holiness, your life's determined purpose will not be for God, but for what you call the evidence of God in your life.[107]

The question for those of us seeking to play for an Audience of One is not so much how to keep ourselves from ever sinning, but what steps to take if and when we do.

Sincerity and Passion Aren't Enough

King David was arguably the most sincere, passionate follower of God ever to have walked the face of the earth. His deepest desire was to please God, regardless of what anyone else thought about him. Yet there were many times in his life when he fell flat on his face. The fact that he was still considered a man after God's own heart says something about the true spiritual journey.

David's affair with Bathsheba wasn't the only time he messed up, either. There was another episode, at the beginning of his reign, when David's shortcomings nearly waylaid him from ever following hard after God again. What made this incident so tough for David was how genuine he had been trying to follow God leading up to the failure. Despite his sincerity, his commitment to God seemed to blow up in his face.

You probably know what this feels like. You come back from a weekend retreat where you've made promises about how your relationship with God is going to be different from now on. And it lasts all the way until Monday morning before you blow it one way or another. Subsequently, you become frustrated and ashamed about how you could crash and burn so soon after a sincere commitment. It's not long before you throw in the towel on the whole enterprise of trying to live wholly for God—until the next inspiring weekend retreat comes along, and then you go through the same steps all over again.

It doesn't have to be like this. David is a living illustration of what it looks like to get back up and keep playing for an Audience of One *after* you blow it—even if it means crawling on your hands and knees to the metaphorical finish line.

Soon after assuming the throne, David conquered the Philistines and made arrangements to bring the recaptured Ark of the Covenant back to Jerusalem. The ark was the most important symbol of God's presence given to Israel. It was the sign that God dwelled with them. David's commitment to bring home the ark was a reflection of his dedication to restore the broken relationship between God and His people.

David loved God. He loved people. And he wanted to bring the two together.

Last minute details for getting the ark ready to make the journey were being handled. The scene was festive with religious fervor:

> They set the ark of God on a new cart....Uzzah and Ahio, sons of Abinadab, were guiding the new cart with the ark of God on it, and Ahio was walking in front of it. David and the whole house of Israel were celebrating with all their might before the Lord, with songs and with harps, lyres, tambourines, sistrums and cymbals.
>
> —2 Sam. 6:3-5

As they started out, not only was David celebrating before the Lord, the whole house of Israel was following suit. This was looking like it would be one of the most glorious days in Israel's history. Not too far into the trek, though, the parade came to a screeching halt:

> When they came to the threshing floor of Nacon, Uzzah reached out and took hold of the ark of God, because the oxen stumbled. The Lord's anger burned against Uzzah because of his irreverent act; therefore God struck him down and he died there beside the ark of God.
>
> —2 Sam. 6:7

There are few stories in the Bible as disturbing as this one. It doesn't seem fair; it doesn't seem to make sense. Everyone was so sincere about what they were doing. Yet their efforts to honor God only incurred His wrath. Uzzah's attempt to protect the ark from falling off the cart resulted in his death. Even David's genuine desire to guide the processional in worship didn't curtail God's judgment. How could God be so harsh when His people were so sincerely and passionately trying to please Him? Isn't that what God wants? Isn't that what it means to play for an Audience of One?

David found out God is looking for more than just sincerity and passion.

Following in the Philistines' Footsteps

What was the problem with David's parade? It may seem like an unimportant detail, but the narrator is careful to repeat that the method David was using to transport the ark was a "new cart." The significance of this detail is lost when you read this story in isolation from the rest of Israel's story. But back in 1 Samuel 6, there was another instance of the ark getting moved from one place to another. On that occasion, it was the Philistines who were transporting it. Notice the method the Philistine leaders prescribed:

> Now then, get a *new cart* ready…take the ark of the Lord and put it on the *cart*.
>
> —1 Sam. 6:7-8, emphasis mine

When David decided to use a "new cart" to bring the ark into Jerusalem, he was following in the Philistines' footsteps. David's mimicking his pagan neighbors was the first sign that this venture wasn't going in the right direction. Of course, from a utilitarian standpoint, there were many reasons David might have chosen a new cart as his mode of transporting the ark:

1. The cart was fast, easy, and convenient.
2. The cart allowed animals, instead of people, to do the burdensome work of pulling the cargo.
3. Perhaps most significantly, Israel had already seen this transportation method work for the Philistines. So why reinvent the wheel?

Why shouldn't David have used a new cart to transport the ark? Because throughout the Law, God was careful to describe how the ark was and was not supposed to be handled. David's real offense was his spiritual ignorance about how to properly transport the ark. God had cautioned Israel about what would happen if anyone (for any reason) touched the holy things:

They must not touch the holy things or they will die.

—Num. 4:15

The question that naturally arises is: *How was David supposed to get the ark to Jerusalem if nobody was allowed to touch it?*
God was fairly clear about that, too:

Cast four gold rings for it and fasten them to its four feet, with two rings on one side and two rings on the other. Then make poles of acacia wood and overlay them with gold. Insert the poles into the rings on the sides of the chest [ark] to carry it.

—Ex. 25:12-15

You can see that by using poles and rings, there was a way to transport the ark without touching it. God's Word outlined precisely how the ark could be carried from one place to another. David simply failed to do his homework on this point. As the king, it was his responsibility to be the spiritual leader of Israel. He wasn't just the commander in chief. It was also his role to know and uphold the Law. His failure in this matter cost Uzzah his life. This tragedy could have been avoided if David had consulted God's Word before launching out to do what seemed like a good idea.

The Religion of Sincerity

There aren't many values that get held up as highly in our culture today as that of sincerity. In many people's eyes, to be sincere is the virtue of all virtues. Being true to oneself has become its own religion. Sincerity is certainly more admirable than duplicity or hypocrisy. But just because one is sincere does not mean one cannot still be sincerely and even dangerously wrong.

The processional looked like it was pleasing to God. But it wasn't. Why? Because it wasn't in line with what God had clearly prescribed in His Word. David sincerely believed he was doing a good thing, but he was sincerely wrong. Sincerity is no substitute for knowing God's Word and obeying it. Ignorance is not bliss. Sometimes, ignorance actually leads to death. The prophets proclaimed this again and again:

> My people perish for a lack of knowledge.
>
> —Hos. 4:6

After all, how can we live a life that is pleasing to God if we don't know what He wants? Asked another way: *How can we love God with all our heart, soul, mind, and strength if we don't know the specific ways He is seeking to be loved?*

David was a man after God's own heart. He was sincere about what he was doing. But the fact that he didn't take the time to find out what God's Word said about how to carry the ark sabotaged his own efforts at trying to please Him. If you want to play for an Audience of One, a key lesson you need to learn is this: *It's impossible to love God if you don't take the time to find out what He wants.*

The same thing is true on a human level: it's tough to love another human being if you don't take the time to find out what he or she wants. In *The Five Love Languages*, Gary Smalley detailed the five pathways through which husbands and wives give and receive love. His conviction was that couples are better able to love each other when they figure out the primary love languages of their spouses. Whether it's "words of encouragement," "quality time," "gifts," "physical touch," or "acts of service,"[108] I've seen marriages significantly helped just because one or both parties in the relationship began speaking the love language that his or her spouse best understood.

Before I was married, my limited experience with the opposite sex led me to assume that giving flowers was the best way to communicate love to women. Then I met Amanda. It didn't take me long to discover she had a sixth love language: *ice cream*. It's not that she didn't enjoy or appreciate getting flowers from me. But the smile on her face and the joy in her voice was a little different when I come home with a pint of her favorite treat. I've learned if I want to show Amanda love the way she wants to be loved, getting her flowers is a sincere gesture, but getting her ice cream is what she really wants. And all I had to do to find out how to better love Amanda was take the time to read the signs. They were all there—expressed in her words and written on her face.

Obedience: God's Primary Love Language

This same principle is true in a relationship with God. If you really want to find out how to love God, all you have to do is take the time to read the signs. They're all there—clearly written in His Word. This simple insight has revolutionized the way I approach reading the Bible. No longer is my quiet time about doing my spiritual exercises, or getting an inspirational thought for the day. Reading the Bible has become a means of getting to know God *so that I can better love Him.*

For example, over the past few years, I've been struck with how much the Bible has to say about God's heart for the poor, how frequently God expresses His concern for the needy and the marginalized, and how often He says our love for the poor is a reflection of our love for Him. Based on this new awareness of what makes God's heart beat faster, my family is investing itself in ministry to the poor in a more intentional way. Don't misunderstand me: our effort to give to the poor is not an attempt to earn God's affections. It's simply flowing out of what I'm finding out about God through His Word. My discovery that caring for the needy is one of God's "love languages" has simply provided us with another pathway through which to express our love for Him.

Conversely, if you neglect God's Word, you short-circuit your ability to love Him because you remain ignorant about how He is seeking to be loved. You may be sincere in your efforts, but sincerity is no substitute for obedience. *Obedience is God's primary love language!* And there's no way to obey what you don't know. David didn't know there was a specific way God wanted to transport the ark, and that's why he blew it. His ignorance on this matter cost Uzzah his life.

When Things Don't Go Your Way

Notice how David reacted to God's judgment:

> Then David was angry because the Lord's wrath had broken out against Uzzah….David was afraid of the Lord that day and said, "How can the ark of the Lord ever come to me?" He was not willing to take the ark of the Lord to be with him….Instead, he took it aside to the house of Obed-Edom.
>
> —2 Sam. 6:8-10

David responded just like some of us do when we've tried to follow God, and things don't work out the way we had hoped: he became angry with God. David actually abandoned the project of bringing the ark into Jerusalem, leaving it at Obed-Edom's house for three months.

> The ark of the Lord remained in the house of Obed-Edom the Gittite for three months, and the Lord blessed him and his entire household.
>
> —2 Sam. 6:11

It was only when David caught wind that the Lord had started blessing the socks off Obed-Edom that he finally realized that perhaps the problem lay with him, not with God or the ark.

What To Do After You Fall

1. Go back to the Bible

What David did next is condensed in 2 Samuel 6 to simply going back to Obed-Edom's house, and retrieving the ark. But in the Chronicles account of this story, we get a more complete picture of what happened before David went back to get the ark:

> Then David summoned Zadok and Abiathar the priests....He said to them, "It was because the Levites did not bring it [the ark] up the first time that the Lord our God broke out in anger against us. We did not inquire of Him how to do it in the prescribed way."
>
> —1 Chron. 15:11-13

At some point during those three months of frustration and confusion, David went back to the Scriptures and discovered the error of his ways. He knew that obedience is God's primary love language, so he went back and found out "the prescribed way" that the job was to be done.

Because spirituality is such a hot topic these days, there are a lot of interesting thoughts floating around out there (and inside us). The Bible is a compass in the stormy sea of religious pluralism. When we're lost, the Word of God will show us the way home. A turning point in John Wesley's life was when he started to see himself as *homo unius libri*—a man of one book. Not that Wesley only studied the Bible. He was actually very well read. But the Scriptures became his true north. The Bible became the plumb line against which everything else was measured:

> My ground is in the Bible. Yea, I am a Bible-bigot. I follow it in all things, both great and small.[109]

If we refuse to get Scripture's perspective, we do so to our peril. God pleads with us:

> If you had responded to my rebuke, I would have poured out my heart to you, and made my thoughts to known to you.
>
> —Prov. 1:23

God deeply desires to pour out His heart to us and make His thoughts known to us, but it's up to us to respond to His rebuke if we want to find our way back home. It's the primary way to hear His voice above the din of our own sincere ideas about how we think things ought to work.

2. *Swallow your pride*

Once he found out what God's Word said about transporting the ark, David was willing to admit he had been wrong. Sometimes it's nothing more than stubborn pride that keeps us from taking this step. We arch our backs, and decide that if we can't follow God perfectly as soon as we set out to do so, we'll just throw in the towel on the whole pursuit. We settle for a nominal Christianity. Some of us choose this kind of relationship with God because constantly having to face the fact that we keep messing up is too discouraging, too tiresome, and too humbling.

The following is supposedly a transcript between a United States naval ship and Canadian authorities off the coast of Newfoundland. It's almost certainly an urban legend, but it's a humorous tale about how pride can so easily block us from admitting we've wandered off course.

Americans: "Please divert your course 15 degrees to the north to avoid a collision."

Canadians: "Recommend you divert your course 15 degrees to the south to avoid a collision."

Americans: "This is the captain of a U.S. Navy ship. I say again, divert your course."

Canadians: "This is but a second class seaman. However, I say again, divert your course."

Americans: "This is the aircraft carrier USS Abraham Lincoln, the second largest ship in the United States' Atlantic fleet. We are accompanied by three destroyers, three cruisers, and numerous support vessels. I demand that you change *your* course 15 degrees north. That's one-five degrees north, or counter measures will be taken to ensure the safety of this ship!"

Canadians: "This is a lighthouse. It's your call!"[110]

The good news for those of us who stray is that anytime we're willing to admit it, God will show us how to get back on the right path. God wants that for us even more than we want it for ourselves. However, He won't force our hand to turn the steering wheel. Like the man in charge of the lighthouse, God says to us, *This is what you need to do to get back on course so you don't shipwreck your faith. But it's your call.*

3.   *Make the necessary course corrections*

David didn't let pride stand in his way. Upon admitting where he had gone wrong, he set out to make the necessary course corrections. He immediately rallied the troops in order to fulfill the original mission of bringing the ark to Jerusalem:

> So the priests and Levites consecrated themselves in order to bring up the ark of the Lord, the God of Israel. And the Levites carried the ark of God with the poles on their shoulders, as Moses had commanded in accordance with the word of the Lord.
>
> —1 Chron. 15:14-15

The fact that David was partially motivated to course correct because he was missing out on a blessing is an example of what God will use to get us back on track. Some of us are so proud that we would rather forego the blessings that come with obedience than have to make the necessary course corrections after we've blown it. Our motives matter, but David's story demonstrates how God condescends to use even our mixed motives to get us to the place where we can hear His voice and obey Him again.

Haven't you ever been inspired to do the right thing because you sensed God's blessings might follow? I have.

In the early days of my recommitment to Christ, my motives for getting into God's Word were far from pure. Basically, I felt inadequate about my knowledge of spiritual things when I was around my new Christian friends—especially when we played Bible Trivia! I hated that game. My ignorance of the Bible made me feel like a second-class Christian around them.

I was particularly insecure around a certain young lady, Larissa, who had caught my eye. I knew that unless I got my spiritual act together, I had no chance of winning her affections. She was going to be a missionary. And if that didn't give me enough of a spiritual inferiority complex, her Bible finished me off. While sitting next to her at church, I stole a glance at her Bible and noticed that its pages had more color than a paint store. At first I thought this was some kind of new, color-coded translation. Then I realized what it meant. She had underlined and highlighted hundreds of Scriptures with a dozen different color-coded pencils. It was further evidence that she would detect my biblical illiteracy as soon as I opened my mouth. This girl knew her Bible.

Motivated by insecurity and inspired by my hope of getting a girlfriend, I decided to begin reading my Bible for fifteen minutes every night before going to bed. I figured it couldn't hurt my cause. (Incidentally, that's all it took to read through the entire Bible in a year: fifteen minutes a day.) I must admit, there were nights when I had no idea what I was reading. But looking back, I know God was at work. It happened without any fanfare, but during my senior year of high school, my mind began to be shaped by the Word of God. By the end of the year, the stories, wisdom, and promises of Scripture had begun to take root in me—such that they were starting to influence how I lived my life.

Motives matter, but God can still work through impure ones. God was more than willing to use my desire for blessing (read: "girlfriend") to get me to a place where I could hear from Him. In fact, it was God's Word that played the most significant role in getting me through an eighteen-month "dark night of the soul" when I got to college. Well-meaning believers didn't know what to say to me as I struggled with mind-crippling doubts and depression. Sermons didn't address what I was going through. The only spiritual counsel that I can remember getting from fellow Christians and even pastors during those days was, "you just need to have more faith."

At some point during those eighteen months, I went back to Job, Jeremiah, and Lamentations. I had vaguely recalled reading through them my senior year of high school. During my first trek through the Bible, though, I considered them irrelevant to my life. Who needed to dwell deeply on such "downer" material? I didn't realize it at the time, but the reason I couldn't relate to Job and Jeremiah was because I was on a spiritual mountaintop during my first year of following Christ. Books like Job and Jeremiah seemed dull and depressing. But I trudged through them anyway—just in case it helped me dazzle my peers the next time we played Bible Trivia!

It's a good thing I read through them.

Two years later, Job and Jeremiah became my patron saints. When I was tempted to throw in the towel on following God, these ancient saints taught me how to be honest with my feelings of despair. They showed me how to keep seeking God despite them. Most importantly, they authenticated my struggle. I realized there were people in the Bible who went through the same spiritual deserts I was going through. Their example inspired me to keep pressing on in my pursuit of God. I'm not sure I would still be following Jesus today if I hadn't come across those often overlooked portions of Scripture.

In a similar way, who knows what might have happened had David not read those seemingly obscure verses about how to transport the ark during those three months when he was angry at God. Those Scriptures instructed him about how to make the necessary course corrections that would lead to blessing and the fulfillment of God's purposes.

4. *Recommit to the journey with all your might*

Once David went back to the Word, admitted where he had gone wrong, and made the necessary course corrections, he took the final step that needs to be taken after we've fallen down. He got back up and recommitted himself to complete the mission God had given him:

> So David went down and brought up the ark of God....When those who were carrying the ark of the Lord had taken six steps, he sacrificed a bull and a fattened calf. David, wearing a linen ephod, danced before

the Lord with all his might, while he and the entire house of Israel brought up the ark of the Lord with shouts and sound of trumpets.

—2 Sam. 6:13-15

Even though David messed up, it didn't stop him from getting up and trying again with all his heart. Sometimes after repenting of our sin, we recommit ourselves to God in a cautiously optimistic kind of way. We're afraid of getting too passionate because we don't want to look like a fool if and when we blow it again. Not so with David. Once he recommitted himself to God, it was all or nothing: David danced before the Lord with *all* his might.

Playing for an Audience of One isn't about achieving absolute perfection. It's about wanting God so badly that we'll do whatever it takes to find out what He wants, and then do it with all our heart—no matter how many times we fall down over the course of our lives. *The saints are those who hobble toward holiness with an insatiable thirst for God.*

I love this definition of a saint because it kicks against the spiritual arrival mentality. I know a woman who loves to talk about how it's been sixty years since she's last sinned in thought, word, or deed. It's true that Jesus came to destroy the works of the devil, one of which is sin, but measuring our sin level is not our calling as Christians. God isn't looking for spiritual superheroes who can boast about how many years it's been since they've last sinned. He wants people who will admit when they blow it, make the necessary course corrections, and keep longing for Him even after they've fallen down again and again and again. That is what playing for an Audience of One is all about: hobbling toward holiness with an insatiable thirst for God.

How Badly Do You Thirst for God?

On a scale of one to ten, how badly do you thirst for God? Before you answer, though, read the story of a young man who left home in an all-out search for God:

He traveled for many weeks in search of a particular spiritual master whom he at last found sitting in prayer beside a river. He begged the man to take him as his disciple.

"Why should I?" the teacher asked.

"I want to find God," the other answered.

Slowly, the master rose to his feet and looked the young man over. "And how badly do want to find God?" he asked.

The other hesitated, not sure how best to answer. But before he could come up with words that seemed appropriate, the master had grabbed his shoulders and dragged him down the bank and into the river, where he held him under the water. Seconds passed, then a minute, then another minute. The young man struggled and kicked, but still the teacher held him down until at last he drew him coughing and gasping out of the water.

"While you were under the water, what was it you wanted?" the teacher asked when he saw that the other was at last able to speak again.

"Air," the young man said, still panting. "Just air."

"And how badly did you want it?"

"All…it was all I wanted in the world. With my whole soul I longed only for air."

"Good," said the teacher. "When there comes a time when you long for God in the same way that you have just now longed for air, come back to me and you will become my disciple."[111]

Do you long for God that way? Do you even measure how you're doing with God based on your longing for Him? Augustine said, "The whole life of the good Christian is one of holy longing."[112] Your relationship with God isn't about sin management. It's not even about sin elimination. Don't get me wrong: sin will be diminished and eventually rooted out of your life as a by-product of your relationship with God. But playing for an Audience of One is primarily about cultivating an insatiable thirst for God, a holy longing for Him.

For some of us the most difficult part of the spiritual journey is what to do the moment we realize we've blown it again. Will our sin cause us to go the way of feeling shame, frustration, anger, and despair—to the point where we throw in the towel on pursuing a life that is wholly pleasing to God? Or will we seek to employ the steps that David took after he messed up:

1. Go back to the Word to get God's perspective on the matter.
2. Admit where we went wrong.
3. Make the necessary course corrections.
4. Recommit to playing for an Audience of One with all our might.

Take a moment to ask yourself which of these steps you're most tempted to ignore when you fall down. Then ask God for help to take that step the next time you need to take it.

Set Free to Bless Our Neighbors

> After he had finished sacrificing the burnt offerings and fellowship offerings, he [David] blessed the people in the name of the Lord Almighty. Then he gave a loaf of bread, a cake of dates and a cake of raisins to each person in the crowd of Israelites.
>
> —2 Sam. 6:17-19

As soon as David finished making sacrifices to God, he turned to his fellow Israelites, who had gathered to see the ark. David's goal in life was not to please people, but he did want to bless them. He longed for them to taste and see that the Lord was good. So what did David do? He gave them a tangible expression of God's love. A loaf of bread, a cake of dates, and some raisins may seem an insignificant gift, but to the people of Israel it was a practical demonstration of God's goodness and provision.

A danger for those of us who strive to play for an Audience of One is we become so concerned not to become distracted by the voices of our neighbors that we end up doing nothing for them. A frequent accusation lobbied against Christians is: *You're so heavenly minded that you're of no earthly good!* If we're unconcerned for those in this world, though, the problem lies not with our being too heavenly minded, but with our being deaf to what heaven actually is calling us to do. God cares deeply about what happens on earth. In fact, those whose ears have been most attuned to the voice of heaven have always been the ones who have made the most significant difference in the world. As C. S. Lewis wrote, "If you read history you will find out that the Christians who did most for the present world were precisely those who thought most of the next."[113]

Playing for an Audience of One does not preclude you from blessing your neighbors. Quite the opposite: it frees you from needing their approval or fearing their censure so you can truly serve them. That's what David was able to do. He cared deeply for people, but without caring deeply what people thought about him. That's the trick.

Tony Campolo is one of my heroes in this regard. He seeks to bless people no matter how it might appear to those looking on from the sidelines. He finds ways to love people for whom others are afraid to get too close. Campolo tells the story:

> I was in Haiti checking on our missionary work. We run seventy-five small schools back in the hills of Haiti. I came to the little Holiday Inn where I always stay and shower and clean up before I board the plane to go home. I left the taxi and was walking to the entrance of the Holiday Inn, when I was intercepted by three girls. I call them girls because the oldest could not have been more than fifteen. And the one in the middle said, "Mister, for ten dollars, I'll do anything you want me to do. I'll do it all night long. Do you know what I mean?"

> I did know what she meant. I turned to the next one and I said, "What about you, could I have you for ten dollars?"

> She said yes. I asked the same of the third girl. She tried to mask her contempt for me with a smile but it's hard to look sexy when you're fifteen and hungry. I said, "I'm in room 210. You be up there in just ten minutes. I have thirty dollars and I'm going to pay for all three of you to be with me all night long."

> I rushed up to the room, called down to the concierge desk, and said, "I want every Walt Disney video you've got in stock." I called down to the restaurant and said, "Do you still make banana splits in this town, because if you do I want banana splits with extra ice cream,

extra everything. I want them delicious, I want them huge, I want four of them!"

The little girls came and the ice cream came and the videos came and we sat at the edge of the bed and we watched the videos and laughed until about one in the morning. That's when the last of them fell asleep across the bed. And as I saw those little girls stretched out asleep on the bed, I thought to myself, nothing's changed, nothing's changed. Tomorrow they will be back on the streets selling their little bodies to dirty, filthy johns because there will always be dirty, filthy johns who for a few dollars will destroy little girls. Nothing's changed.

I didn't know enough Creole to tell them about the salvation story, but the word of the Spirit said this: *But for one night, for one night you let them be little girls again.*[114]

Many Christians lambasted Campolo for doing something that could have been perceived as impropriety. I recently visited a Web site that invested pages of cyber ink cataloging all of the things Campolo did wrong during this visit to Haiti. Ironically, this particular Christian ministry that maligned Campolo is having no impact on the impoverished people of Haiti. Yet they felt compelled to take issue with Campolo's ministry of ice cream sundaes and Disney movies. It was fascinating to read their editorial pot shots lobbed from the safety of their seats in the grandstands of religiosity.

There will always be religious watchdogs who care a lot about how things appear, but who care very little about people. Tony Campolo decided long ago not to be concerned with what people thought about him. He'd rather spend his energy showing real compassion for real people as an expression of his real love for God. Like the bread, dates, and raisins David offered the people of Israel, even ice cream sundaes and a good night's sleep can be a tangible expression of God's blessing when it flows out of a heart bent on pleasing Jesus.

A Prophet Is Without Honor in His Own Hometown

The greatest test of David's heart for God, though, was still waiting for him at home:

> As the ark of the Lord was entering the City of David, Michal
> daughter of Saul watched from a window. And when she saw King
> David leaping and dancing before the Lord, she despised him in her
> heart....When David returned home to bless his household, Michal
> daughter of Saul came out to meet him and said, "How the king of
> Israel has distinguished himself today, disrobing in the sight of the
> slave girls of his servants as any vulgar fellow would!"
>
> —2 Sam. 6:16, 20

Three times in this brief episode (6:16, 20, 23) the narrator refers to
Michal as the "daughter of Saul." The author's intent is that we see her
through the same set of lenses that we viewed her father. Michal and Saul
shared the same character flaw. Just like her father, the voice of Michal's
neighbors was louder in her ears than was the voice of God.

Michal "despised" David because she was ashamed of how priestly
he was becoming in his kingly duties. Her concern was not about
modesty. She was not taking issue with David dancing before the ark
in his underwear, as most sermons on this passage propose. Michal was
upset because he had taken off his royal robe, which was the marker
that identified him as the *king*. In its place David wore a linen ephod,
the recognized attire of a *priest*.

Wearing the ephod was David's way of demonstrating his willingness
to live out his calling as a priest for God's people. He wanted to lead the
people of Israel in worship. But Michal wasn't interested in being married
to a *priest*. She wanted to be associated with the power and prestige of a
king. Michal was embarrassed that David had humbled himself to such
a low estate, when as the king he should have been concerned about
looking like royalty.

Dancing for the Lord

David's response to Michal serves as the climax to the story:

> I will celebrate before the Lord. I will become even more undignified
> than this, and I will be humiliated in my own eyes.
>
> —2 Sam. 6:21-22

It wasn't just that David didn't care what his wife thought. It's that he cared so much more about what God thought. It was before the *Lord* that David was dancing! Whereas Michal was obsessed by how the crowd might perceive her husband without his royal garb, David lived by St. Francis of Assisi's advice, "wearing the world like a loose garment, which touches us in a few places and there lightly."[115]

David wasn't dancing for the people of Israel, and he wasn't dancing for his wife either. Five times he was said to be dancing before the *Lord* (v5, 14, 16, 21a, 21b). David knew, as the Chinese proverb says, "Those who hear not the music think the dancer mad!" He didn't care what people thought about him. He was listening to the tune God was playing, and moving to the rhythm of that music regardless of how his dancing looked to anyone else.

Vindication

The final verse of 2 Samuel 6 serves as the epilogue to the story:

Michal daughter of Saul had no children to the day of her death.
—2 Sam. 6:23

Barrenness was frequently (though not always) a punishment for sin. In this case, God was judging Michal on the grounds of her religion of image management. She was consumed with her reputation. The fruit didn't fall far from the tree. The connection between Michal following in the footsteps of her father, Saul, and the judgment she incurred was unmistakable.

The judgment leveled against Michal was also about vindicating David. It served as a reminder that God ultimately defends those who dance before Him, regardless of what anyone (even your loved ones) think. Playing for an Audience of One can be lonely at times. There will be moments when you will be misunderstood, times when your obedience may look foolish to outsiders, and occasions when even those closest to you will ridicule you for what appears to be spiritual recklessness.

Be careful about spending too much energy trying to justify yourself before these people. There may be times when it is appropriate to stand up and defend your actions. David responded to his wife's accusations, but only briefly. Too often, playing defense attorney for ourselves becomes a fulltime job, and distracts us from staying focused on what we need to be doing. Augustine's prayer is an appropriate one for those of us who tend to practice law without a license: "O Lord, deliver me from the lust of always trying to vindicate myself."[116]

God's vindication will come...eventually.

We all have moments when we deeply desire to be vindicated: someone else gets credit for work we've done, we get blamed for something for which we were not at fault, our motives get called into question when they were pure, or we're mocked by those who hear us talk about the hope we have within us. The list goes on and on. Sometimes the vindication we seek is over something unimportant and petty. But at other times, it's over a matter of eternal significance.

What do you do with your craving for vindication? If you want to follow in David's footsteps, then work it out in God's presence. Like David, pray your desire for vindication:

> May my vindication come from You; may Your eyes see what is right.
>
> —Ps. 17:2
>
> Vindicate me, O Lord!
>
> —Ps. 26:1

Praying for God's vindication is a means of appropriately channeling our deep-seated cravings for personal justice. It is an act of trust that eventually God will set things right. Praying for vindication (instead of arguing for it) also keeps us focused on our commitment to listen for God's approval over and against the approval of our fellow human beings. Although we long for certain people to validate us where we've been wronged, ultimately only God's validation will satisfy. That's why it's so important not to put the desire for vindication on earth ahead of the vindication that will come in heaven. After all, anytime we reach for something on earth that is intended to be ours in heaven, we run the risk of forfeiting God's best gift to us. As C.S. Lewis writes:

But what, you ask, of earth? Earth, I think, will not be found by anyone to be in the end a very distinct place. I think earth, if chosen instead of heaven, will turn out to have been, all along, only a region of hell; and earth, if put second to heaven, to have been from the beginning a part of heaven itself.[117]

The Ultimate Moment of Approval

There will be no more satisfying moment for those who put earth second to heaven than when we hear the words we have longed to hear our whole lives:

> Well done, good and faithful servant! You have been faithful with a few things; I will put you in charge of many things. Come and share your Master's happiness!
>
> —Matt. 25:23

No longer will we be tempted to give in to the luring voices that distract us from listening to God. The voice of the One we have longed to hear will sing so clearly in our ears that the beat of our heart will follow in perfect time. In that moment, we will realize that all the times we chose to play for an Audience of One were completely worth it.

Randy Alcorn's depiction of this first moment of eternity inspires me to stay the course:

> The multitudes innumerable began to sing the song for which they had been made, a song that echoed off a trillion planets and reverberated in a quadrillion places in every nook and cranny of the creation's expanse. Audience and orchestra and choir all blended into one great symphony, one grand cantata of rhapsodic melodies and sustaining harmonies. All were participants. Only One was an Audience, the Audience of One. The smile of the King's approval swept through the choir like fire across dry wheat fields.
>
> When the song was complete, the Audience of One stood and raised his great arms, then clapped his scarred hands together in thunderous applause, shaking the ground and sky, jarring every corner of the cosmos. His applause went on and on, unstopping and unstoppable.

Every one…realized something with undiminished clarity in that instant. They wondered why they had not seen it all along. What they knew in that moment, in every fiber of their beings, was that this Person and this Place were all they had ever longed for…and ever would.[118]

Between now and when that glorious forever begins, keep seeking to play for the Audience of One—even if you fall down again and again, and have to crawl on your hands and knees to the finish line. In the end, it will be worth it!

Prayer of a Hobbler

Come, thou Fount of every blessing, tune my heart to sing Thy grace… O to grace how great a debtor daily I'm constrained to be! Let thy goodness, like a fetter, bind my wandering heart to thee. Prone to wander, Lord, I feel it, prone to leave the God I love; Here's my heart, O take and seal it, seal it for thy courts above.[119]

—Come Thou Fount of Every Blessing (v3)

Going Deeper

1. Come up with a Bible reading plan so as to guard yourself against sincere spiritual ignorance. Be specific:
   a. When during the day will you read? Before breakfast, during lunch break, right before bed? There's no right or wrong time. Just set a time and keep to it.
   b. What will you read?
      • Reading through the Bible in a year means reading about three chapters a day. It only takes about fifteen minutes a day to reach this goal.
      • Do a topical study: using a concordance, look up Scriptures that speak to an area with which you need God's help. For example: gossip, courage, anxiety, purity, etc.
      • Do a book-study: reading and meditating on one chapter a day will get you through books like 1 Samuel, Proverbs, the Gospel of John, or Acts in a month or less.
   c. Decide how long you will keep this reading plan. Change it up. Variety is a good thing.

2. When you fall short of playing for an Audience of One, you will be tempted to throw in the towel. Remember to employ the steps David took after he messed up:
   • Go back to the Word to get God's perspective on the matter
   • Admit where you went wrong
   • Make the necessary course corrections
   • Recommit yourself to following God with all your heart
   If you know one of these steps will be difficult for you, take some time right now to pray about it. Then commit yourself to keeping that particular step at the forefront of your thinking and praying over the next leg of your marathon journey.

3. Memorize one of David's prayers for vindication to prepare yourself for those moments when you're tempted to play "defense attorney." (Psalm 17:2 or 26:1)

'PLAYING FOR AN AUDIENCE OF ONE' COVENANT

"Am I now trying to win the approval of men, or of God?"
—Galatians 1:10

- I will stand up for the truth even if it means being the lone voice in the matter. I will not let the fear of people silence me when I need to speak up.
- I will let Jesus' love for me shape the way I view myself, and reject the lie that 'Who I am' = 'My performance' + 'Other people's opinions of me.'
- I will surrender myself, my abilities, and anything else "in my hand" to God, trusting that He can do all He wants to do through me once I am yielded to Him.
- I will accept the fact that Jesus' primary purpose for my life is not to make me happy, but to make me holy. No matter how much it hurts, I will not let apparent failure dissuade me from doing what God calls me to do.
- I will play second fiddle with grace no matter how much my ego kicks against it, trusting that there is nothing God can't do through me so long as I don't care who gets the credit.
- I will live my life with the conviction that there is sufficient time to do the whole will of God, but also with the understanding that following Jesus sometimes means saying 'no' to good people and good causes.
- I will become a Levite: transferring the title of all my money and possessions into Jesus' name, tithing as a first step on the stewardship journey, and then staying attentive and responsive to how God wants me to use the other 90%.
- I will allow God's gracious warnings regarding 'the price tag for playing for the crowd' to guard my heart from going the way of people pleasing.
- I will press on in my relationship with God after I blow it. I will go back to the Word to get God's perspective, admit where I went wrong, make the necessary course corrections, and then recommit myself to playing for an Audience of One with all my heart.
- I will wait for vindication to come from God, and resign from playing 'defense attorney' every time I am wronged or misunderstood.

Sources

~~%~~

Chapter 1: *"The Stakes Are Higher Than You Think"*

1. Roland Bainton, *Here I Stand: A Life of Martin Luther.* Nashville, Tennessee: Abingdon Press, 1978, 144. I first read this story in Oswald Sanders, *Spiritual Leadership.* Chicago, Illinois: Moody Press, 1994, 60. Sanders quotes James Burns, *Revivals, Their Laws and Leaders.* London: Hoddler & Stroughton, 1909, 167-68.
2. Ajith Fernando, *NIV Application Commentary on Acts.* Grand Rapids, Michigan: Zondervan, 1998, 161. Fernando quotes William Barclay, *The Acts of the Apostles.* Saint Andrew: Edinburgh, 1976, 41.
3. C.S. Lewis, *Weight of Glory.* New York, New York: MacMillan Publishing, 1980, 11-12.
4. Dr. Samuel Johnson: Quoted in C.S. Lewis, *Mere Christianity.* New York, New York: MacMillan Publishing, 1960, 78.

Chapter 2: *"Though None Go With Me, Still I Will Follow"*

5. Two years later, the denominational leaders made the following change to its membership covenant in order to reflect a move to a principle-based membership model: *"In essence, the Covenant moved from a legal base (with a longer list of specific behaviors and*

attitudes) to a principle base (with a shorter list of guiding, overarching principles)." —2003 Free Methodist Book of Discipline, Par 3500 A.

6. Gordon Fee, "Lecture on Galatians." Regent College, Vancouver, B.C., 2002.

7. Robert Kriegel and David Brandt, *Sacred Cows Make the Best Burger*. Warner Books, 1996.

8. Swindoll, *Living Above the Level of Mediocrity*. Nashville, Tennessee: The W Publishing Group, 1989, 225-226.

9. Oswald Sanders, *Spiritual Leadership*. Chicago, Illinois: Moody Press, 1994, 118. Sanders quotes A.W. Tozer.

10. Jon Johnston, *You Can Stand Strong in the Face of Fear*. Wheaton, Illinois: Victor Books, 1990, 56-58.

11. Gordon Fee, "Lecture on Galatians." Regent College, Vancouver, B.C., Spring 2002.

12. A.W. Tozer, *The Pursuit of God*. Camp Hill, Pennsylvania: Christian Publication, Inc., 1993, 133-134.

13. Ibid., 134-135.

Chapter 3: *"The Disciple Jesus Loved"*

14. John Ortberg, *The Life You've Always Wanted*. Grand Rapids, Michigan: Zondervan, 1997, 161.

15. Author unknown. Paraphrased from a forwarded e-mail a friend sent me.

16. John 13:23; 19:26; 20:2; 21:7, 20.

17. Beth Moore, *The Beloved Disciple*. Nashville, Tennessee: Broadman and Holman Publishers, 2003, 126-128.

18. Demotivators Calendar, 2002. The Demotivator Calendar is a product of Despair Inc., Austin, Texas.

19. Brennan Manning, *Ragamuffin Gospel*. Sisters, Oregon: Multnomah Books, 1990, 165.

20. Brennan Manning, *Abba's Child*. Colorado Springs, Colorado: NavPress, 2002, 64.

21. Brennan Manning, *Ragamuffin Gospel*. Sisters, Oregon: Multnomah Books, 1990, 208.

22. Robert McGee, *Search for Significance*. Nashville, Tennessee: The W Publishing Group, 2003, 53-55.
23. A.W. Tozer, *The Pursuit of God*. Camp Hill, PA: Christian Publication, Inc., 1993, 142.
24. Richard Swenson, *Margin*. Colorado Springs, Colorado: NavPress, 1992, 231. Swenson quotes Thomas a Kempis, *Imitation of Christ*, trans. Richard Whitford (New York: Washington Square Press, 1953 [written in 1424]), 13.
25. John Ortberg, *The Life You've Always Wanted*. Grand Rapids, Michigan: Zondervan, 1997, 152. Ortberg quotes Henri Nouwen, *Return of the Prodigal*. New York, New York: Doubleday, 1992, 42.
26. Brennan Manning, *Abba's Child*. Colorado Springs, Colorado: NavPress, 2002, 35.
27. Richard A. Swenson, *Margins*. Colorado Springs, Colorado: NavPress, 1992, 231.
28. Brennan Manning, *Signature of Jesus*. Sister, Oregon, Multnomah Books, 1996, 103-105.

Chapter 4: *"What's in Your Hand?"*

29. Brennan Manning, *Ragamuffin Gospel*. Sisters, Oregon: Multnomah Books, 1990, 178. Manning quotes Nikos Kazantzakis from *Report to Greco: The Prologue*.
30. John Ortberg, *God Is Closer Than You Think*. Grand Rapids, Michigan: Zondervan, 2005, 64. Ortberg quotes Brother Lawrence, *Practicing the Presence of God*. Springdale, Pennsylvania: Whitaker House, 1982, 36.
31. Brennan Manning, *Abba's Child*. Colorado Springs, Colorado: NavPress, 2002, 50. Manning quotes John Eagan, *A Traveler Toward the Dawn*. Chicago, Illinois: Loyola University Press, 1990, xii.
32. Oswald Chambers, *My Utmost for His Highest*. Grand Rapids, Michigan: Discovery House Publishers, 1992, January 15.
33. Ibid., January 15.
34. C.S. Lewis, *Great Divorce*. New York, New York: MacMillan Publishing, 1946, 72.

35. Randy Alcorn, *The Treasure Principle*. Sisters, Oregon: Multnomah Publishers, 2001, 55. Alcorn quotes A.W. Tozer, "The Transmutation of Wealth," *Born After Midnight*. Harrisburg, Pennsylvania: Christian Publications, 1959, 107.

36. Oswald Chambers, *My Utmost for His Highest*. Grand Rapids, Michigan: Discovery House Publishers, 1992, January 1.

37. John Wesley. As quoted by John Telford, ed, *The Letters of John Wesley*, A.M. 8 Volumes. London: The Epworth Press, 1931, 6:272.

38. Ajith Fernando, NIV *Application Commentary on Acts*. Grand Rapids, Michigan: Zondervan, 1998, 161.

Chapter 5: *"Sometimes Faithfulness Leads to 'Failure'"*

39. Dixon Hoste. Quoted by Oswald Sanders, *Spiritual Leadership*. Chicago, Illinois: Moody Press, 1994, 118.

40. Michael Jordan, one of his Nike shoe advertisements.

41. Brennan Manning, *Ragamuffin Gospel*. Sisters, Oregon: Multnomah Books, 1990, 135. Manning paraphrases T.S. Eliot on this point.

42. Oswald Chambers, *My Utmost for His Highest*. Grand Rapids, Michigan: Discovery House Publishers, 1992, January 11.

43. Ibid., January 11.

44. Ibid., Oct 1.

45. Charles Swindoll, *Paul, A Man of Grace and Grit*. Nashville, Tennessee: The W Publishing Group, 2002, 1-2.

46. Herman Melville. This quote was found at www.KnowProSE.com.

47. Mother Theresa. This story was found at www.personal-development.com.

48. William Tyndale. I don't remember where I found this quote, but I was struck enough by it that I copied it down into my prayer journal years ago.

49. Martin Luther King, Jr. This quote was found at www.members.aol/klove01/marquote.htm.

50. John Ortberg, *God Is Closer Than You Think*. Grand Rapids, Michigan: Zondervan, 2005, 138. Ortberg quotes Brother

Lawrence, *Practicing the Presence of God*. Springdale, Pennsylvania: Whitaker House, 1982, 45.

51. Ajith Fernando, *NIV Application Commentary on Acts*. Grand Rapids, Michigan: Zondervan, 1998, 288-289.

52. Charles Swindoll, *Paul, A Man of Grace and Grit*. Nashville, Tennessee: The W Publishing Group, 2002, 92.

53. Abraham Kuyper. This quote was found at www.menformodern-reformation.org.

54. *Transformations*. Directed by George Otis, Jr. Sentinel Group, 1999. I don't agree with everything purported in this documentary, nor has every claim in the video been corroborated. Nonetheless, Pastor Julio Ruibal's witness for Jesus and his influence on the world is unquestioned.

55. Ajith Fernando, *NIV Application Commentary on Acts*. Grand Rapids, Michigan: Zondervan, 1998, 268. Fernando quotes early church father Tertullian (160-225 A.D.), *Apology*, Chapter 50.

56. Oswald Sanders, *Spiritual Leadership*. Chicago, Illinois: Moody Press, 1994, 121.

Chapter 6: *"Playing Second Fiddle"*

57. Charles Swindoll, *Paul, A Man of Grace and Grit*. Nashville, Tennessee: The W Publishing Group, 2002, 109.

58. Oswald Sanders, *Spiritual Leadership*. Chicago, Illinois: Moody Press, 1994, 52.

59. Ibid, 62.

60. Bobb Biehl, *Mentoring*. Nashville, Tennessee: Broadman and Holman Publishers, 1996, 60-61.

Chapter 7: *"Even Jesus Said No"*

61. Oswald Sanders, *Spiritual Leadership*. Chicago, Illinois: Moody Press, 1994, 94.

62. 2006 Government Study on Time: US Department of Labor, Bureau of Labor Statistics on the American Use of Time. www.bls.gov/newsrelease/atus.nr0.htm.

63. Oswald Sanders, *Spiritual Leadership*. Chicago, Illinois: Moody Press, 1994, 96.

64. Brennan Manning, *Abba's Child*. Colorado Springs, Colorado: NavPress, 2002, 34.

65. Dallas Willard, *Renovation of the Heart*. Colorado Springs, Colorado: NavPress, 2002, 152-153.

66. Paraphrased from a letter written by a Catholic priest to his fellow priests. One of the professors from Asbury Seminary, Dr. Brian Dodd, handed it out during a lecture on time management. The author's name was not mentioned in the letter.

67. Found at NET Bible: Sermon Illustrations. www.net.bible.org/illustration.php?topic=565. The Web site cited Henry Ford's quote from Bits & Pieces, Sept. 19, 1991, 18.

68. Oswald Sanders, *Spiritual Leadership*. Chicago, Illinois: Moody Press, 1994, 97.

69. Ibid., 117.

70. Ibid., 91.

71. Robert McGee, *Search for Significance*. Nashville, Tennessee: The W Publishing Group, 2003, 37.

72. I found this quote under a category entitled, "Quotes on Ego." www.storytellingmonk.org/ref/quotes/ego.htm.

Chapter 8: *"Transferring the Title"*

73. Peter Kim and James Patterson's work is cited by Bill Hybels, *Becoming a Contagious Christian*. Grand Rapids, Michigan: Zondervan, 1994, 121.

74. Robert Wuthnow, *God and Mammon in America*. New York, New York: MacMillan Publishing, 1994, 150-151.

75. John L. Ronsvalle and Sylvia Ronsvalle, *The State of Church Giving Through 2000*. Champaign, Illinois: Empty Tomb, 2002, 40. This statistic was cited on Generous Giving's website at www.generousgiving.org.

76. Ron Sider, *Rich Christians in an Age of Hunger*. Downers Grove, Illinois, Inter-Varsity Press, 1980, 58. Sider quotes Luther from *Post-American*, I, No. 4 (Summer 1972), p1.

77. "Donald Trump," *US News & World Report*, 1/9/89. I first discovered this quote from Net Bible: Sermon Illustrations. www. net.bible.org/illustration.php?topic=1761.

78. Net Bible: Sermon Illustrations. www.net.bible.org/illustration. php?topic=1761.

79. "The Voice in the Wilderness," quoted in *Discipleship Journal*, Issue 53, 1989, 21.

80. Randy Alcorn, *Treasure Principle*. Sisters, Oregon: Multnomah Publishers, 2001, 59.

81. Net Bible: Sermon Illustrations. www.net.bible.org/illustration. php?topic=1761.

82. Bill Hybels, *Courageous Leadership*. Grand Rapids, Michigan: Zondervan, 2002, 98.

83. Randy Alcorn, *Treasure Principle*. Sisters, Oregon: Multnomah Publishers, 2001, 55. Alcorn quotes A. W. Tozer, *The Transmutation of Wealth*, "Born after Midnight," 107.

84. Randy Alcorn, *The Treasure Principle*. Sisters, Oregon: Multnomah Publishers, 2001, 73.

85. W. Graham Scroggie quote found at Net Bible: Sermon Illustrations. www.net.bible.org/illustration.php?topic=1761.

86. Erwin McManus, *Uprising*. Nashville, Tennessee: Thomas Nelson Publishers, 2003, 170-171.

87. Albert Outler, *John Wesley's Sermons*. Nashville, Tennessee: Abingdon, 1991, 351-355.

88. Ancient Irish Hymn, Public Domain.

Chapter 9: *"Playing for the Crowd"*

89. J.H. Jewett, as quoted by Oswald Sanders, *Spiritual Leadership*. Chicago, Illinois: Moody Press, 1994, 49.

90. Cited from http://en.wikiquote.org/wiki/Sally_Field.

91. Richard Swenson, *Margin*. Colorado Springs, Colorado: NavPress, 1992, 231.

92. Henri Nouwen, *Sabbatical Journey: The Diary of his Final Year*. New York, New York: the Crossroad Publishing Company, 1998, viii. I first read this story in John Ortberg's *If You Want to Walk on*

Water, You've Got to Get Out of the Boat. Grand Rapids, Michigan: Zondervan, 2001, 182.

93. Ajith Fernando, NIV *Application Commentary on Acts.* Grand Rapids, Michigan: Zondervan, 1998, 161. Fernando quotes William Barclay, The Acts of the Apostles. Saint Andrew: Edinburgh, 1976, 41.

94. Daniel Goleman, *Emotional Intelligence.* New York, New York: Bantam Books, 1995, 80.

95. Ibid., 80.

96. Robert Dugan, *Winning the New Civil War*, 25-27. Dugan cites Aleksandr Solzhenitsyn's *The Gulag Archipelago.* I first read this story on Net Bible: Sermon Illustrations. www.net.bible.org/illustration.php?topic=180.

97. I found this story on NET Bible: Sermon Illustrations. www.net.bible.org/illustration.php?topic=180.

98. Philip Yancey, *Rumors of Another World.* Grand Rapids, Michigan: Zondervan, 2003, 220.

99. Brennan Manning, *Ruthless Trust.* New York, New York: Harper Collins, 2000, 121.

100. J.H. Jewett, as quoted by Oswald Sanders, *Spiritual Leadership.* Chicago, Illinois: Moody Press, 1994, 49.

101. A.W. Tozer, *The Pursuit of God.* Camp Hill, Pennsylvania: Christian Publication, Inc., 1993, 145, 146

102. Samuel Brengle, as quoted by Oswald Sanders, *Spiritual Leadership.* Chicago, Illinois: Moody Press, 1994, 62.

103. A.W. Tozer, *Pursuit of God.* Camp Hill, Pennsylvania: Christian Publication, Inc., 146.

Chapter 10: *"Hobbling Toward Holiness"*

104. Elliot Wright, *The Holy Company: Christian Heroes and Heroines.* New York, New York: MacMillan Publishing Company, Inc., 1980, 1.

105. Terry Fisher, San Mateo, California. Quoted in *Preaching Resources*, Spring 1996, 69.

106. Oswald Chambers, *My Utmost for His Highest.* Grand Rapids, Michigan: Discovery House Publishers, 1992, November 15.

107. Ibid., December 2.

108. Gary Smalley, *The Five Love Languages*. Chicago, Illinois: Northfield Publishing, 2004.
109. John Wesley, *The Works of John Wesley*. Grand Rapids, Michigan: Zondervan, 1958, Volume 5: 169.
110. I first heard this story in a sermon being told as though it was based on an actual transcript from the Navy. But it's almost certainly an urban legend, as this website suggests: www.snopes.com/military/lighthouse.asp.
111. Ernest Boyer, Jr. *Finding God at Home*. New York, New York: Harper Collins, 1998, 27-28.
112. Augustine. I first read this quote in John Eldredge, *The Journey of Desire*. Nashville, Tennessee: Thomas Nelson, 2000.
113. C.S. Lewis, *Mere Christianity*. New York, New York: MacMillan Publishing Company, Inc., 1952, 118.
114. Tony Campolo, *Doing Greater Things*. Radio Program #4001, Air Date 10/6/96.
115. Dallas Willard, *Renovation of the Heart*. Colorado Springs, Colorado: NavPress, 2002, 72.
116. Augustine. I saw this quote at www.sermonillustrations.com/a-z/c/criticism.htm.
117. C.S. Lewis, *Great Divorce*. New York, New York: MacMillan Publishing Company, 1946, 7.
118. Randy Alcorn, *Safely Home*. Carol Stream, Illinois: Tyndale House, 2001, 394-95.
119. Robert Robinson, *Come Thou Fount of Every Blessing*, 1735-1790, Public Domain.

Printed in the United States
125024LV00002B/355-423/P